Dedicated to:

I would like to thank all the people that helped me with this book, but I can't. I did it all myself. Of course that's not true. It took a LOT of help.

Joy McGay for her encouragement.

Janet Pless for always telling me "Butch you should write a book".

To my wife, Diana, for being the second reader and first technical editor.

To daughter Sherri and son Cary for their technical help.

And of course to my Big Brother Jack.

To everyone who crossed my path both good and bad, happy and sad.

A special thanks to my Lord and Savior without who's help I would not have been able to write a single word.

Suggested reading: John 3:16, Romans 3:23

Thank you for a not so common life.

ISBN 978-0-692-34988-5 $15.95
(2nd Printing - December 2014)   SmokingDuck.Net

Copyright © 2014 By Ronald E. Vaughn
All Rights Reserved

INTRODUCTION

*** BUTCH ***

I really don't know where to start telling you about my friend Butch. He really isn't anyone special. He is just your average guy that has had a not so average life. Not so average if you consider knowing people that committed suicide and murder, throw in a touch of romance, a smidgeon of humor and some sadness, with a sort of Huckleberry Finn beginning. You've pretty much got Butch!

CHAPTER ONE

THE BIG EVENT

December the 7th, 1941, Japan bombed Pearl Harbor and World War II was declared. In 1941 gas was nineteen cents per gallon, milk thirty-four cents a gallon, U.S. Postage stamp three cents, the average house cost six thousand nine hundred dollars, and a loaf of bread eight cents. In 1941 one dollar would buy the same as sixteen dollars one cent in 2014.

The real big event of 1941 was on October 15th, at Women's Hospital in Flint, Michigan, an eight pound eight ounce baby boy named Ronald came into the world kicking and screaming. When Harold, Butch's dad, first saw him he said, "Look at that chubby kid, he looks madder than hell!" Then he said, "Hello Butch." The nickname stayed with Butch the rest of his life. Butch pretty much lived up to that name ever since.

Butch asked his mother why he was born at the Women's Hospital.

Butch got an answer that he didn't expect. His mother said the delivering doctor practiced at St. Joseph Hospital and Women's Hospital. Edna heard if there was a troubled delivery, which in 1941 was not all that uncommon, and there had to be a choice between the life of the baby and that of the mother, St. Joseph chooses the life of the baby. Women's Hospital chooses the life of the mother. Hence, Butch was born at Women's Hospital. You wonder what would have happened to ole Butch if he was born now with abortion and all? Maybe Butch was an afterthought or a whoops!

The family was Harold (dad), Edna (ma), and Jack, Butch's eleven year older brother.

CHAPTER TWO

*** THE FOLKS ***

*** HAROLD ***

Harold was born on a farm in Terra Haute, Indiana in 1907. He was the third child of Joe and Ollie's five boys and two girls.

Ollie's family were successful farmers in the area. Ollie's father gave each child a good start in married life. Each child received forty acres of land, a cow, pigs, a few chickens and a mule to start farming.

Unfortunately, Joe was not a successful farmer nor did he know much about business. He was always on the verge of losing the farm. When the boys got old enough they had to work.

At seventeen Harold quit school to help his father in one of

4

Joe's business ventures. Joe bid and received a contract with the local school to transport kids from the country to school. There wasn't any motorized school buses then. They used mules hitched up to long enclosed wood wagons that had windows on the sides. The children sat along the sides around the wood fired stove. Joe drove one team, Harold the other.

In time, Harold and his older brother Clarence started off for the auto plants up north in Michigan. Any location north of where you are is referred to as 'up north'. Harold and Clarence had friends that were already working for General Motors in Flint, Michigan. They started out walking, then hitchhiking, and later jumping a train. Eventually, they both arrived in Flint, also got jobs at GM, and sent for their families.

After a few months something happened. No one knows exactly what, but Harold quit his job at General Motors. Shortly after Harold hired in, there was a difference of opinion between GM and Harold and Harold lost. Harold held a number of jobs, some in the machine shop business learning to run lathes and mills. Then he met and married Edna.

*** EDNA ***

Edna was raised in a small country town. Her father died when she was very young, leaving five girls and one boy for her mother to raise. Edna's mother, Carrie, worked in a laundry making barely minimum wage. As soon as the girls and their brother turned sixteen they quit school and went to work to help pay the bills. Edna joined her mother and sisters in the laundry.

Edna met and married Harold when she was nineteen. Shortly after marriage, she gave birth to Jack.

The depression of 1930 came. Edna never trusted banks. She never put her money in any bank. She kept cold cash in shoe boxes, under mattresses, anywhere but banks. She paid cash for what she bought. No credit. Risk nothing.

JACK

Jack was the kid all parents would want. He was a very good student, B plus all the way. The teachers all liked him. Jack, although not big in stature, was an outstanding athlete. He lettered four years in varsity football, basketball, track, and baseball. He also had the lead in school plays.

6

Right after high school Jack was drafted into the Marine Corp. During the Korean War he rose to the rank of buck sergeant in just under two years. Jack was lucky he did not have to go to Korea. Butch looked up to Jack as if he were some kind of god. Butch would tell people, "My brother Jack can do this, and my brother Jack can do that."

Jack did keep Butch out of trouble most of the time. Butch would bite off more than he could chew in a fight, usually with someone older and bigger, and Jack would bail him out. He taught Butch how to play all the sports. Butch was just not as good as Jack, but he did okay.

CHAPTER THREE

*** THE COMMUNITY ***

Butch was brought home from the hospital to the community as it was called, more exact the Utley community. The streets where Butch lived were made of gravel, and were dirty and dusty in the summer, snowy and icy in the winter, muddy and wet in the spring. The houses in the neighborhood were small, old wood frames, but well kept. The Utley community was made up of hard working people, a real hodgepodge of families, mainly poor. Most of the men in the community worked at General Motors, known in the Flint area as 'Generous Motors'. The women, for the most part, stayed home and took care of the kids. Years later Jack asked Butch, "Did you know we were poor?" Butch said, "It didn't seem poor to me as everyone around us were the same."

Right in the middle of the community was everyone's pride and joy, the Utley School, kindergarten through twelve. The school building was not a nice red brick building like most of the schools in the city of Flint. Utley's school building was a two-story wood frame

8

structure, painted white. It was hot in the early fall and spring, and cold in the winter. The entire enrollment of the school was approximately four hundred students.

A lot of the families in the Utley community, like Butch's family, came from out of state. One section of Utley was called little Missouri. One was called the Augusta Street Rats, another the Utley Angels.

No matter what section of the Utley community you came from, they were all honest, hard working people, proud of their community and even prouder of their country. Most of the Utley community boys would not go to college. None would join the National Guard or move to Canada to evade the draft, and you better not let anyone know if you did. They loved their country and were proud to be American. When they heard God Bless America or the Star Spangled Banner everyone stood and the men removed their hats. They all knew the words to the song. They didn't necessarily agree on what was going on in government, but they knew it was the best government in the world. Think maybe we've lost something there?

*** THE HOUSE ***

Butch's family's house was a single-story twenty-four by thirty-two feet wood frame built on a cement slab, no basement, no bathroom, no hot water. Central heat? No! Only a large oil space heater in the living room. The rest of the house was heated by gravity heat. What was gravity heat? You hoped the warm air would float into the other rooms. When it really got cold, ten above to zero degrees, Butch's mom, all four foot ten inches of her, would hang blankets over the archways leading out of the living room into other rooms, trying to trap all the heat she could for the living area and two bedrooms. Yes, only two bed rooms for the four of them.

*** THE OLE TWO-HOLER ***

Bathroom? Wasn't any. Not inside anyway. There was the outhouse. If you never went to the toilet in an outhouse, you just haven't been to the toilet! The outhouse was a wooden structure about eight feet long, six feet wide and six feet tall, one door in front. It was hot in the summer, and the hotter it got the more it stunk. Butch says it stunk so bad the smell would gag a maggot in a gut wagon. In the winter if it was ten degrees outside it was ten degrees inside. Butch once said the outhouse got so cold that it would pucker your butt hole up like a snare drum.

Inside the outhouse was a bench, the bench was the width of the toilet, about three feet high and about two feet deep with a top on it and two or three holes cut into the bench. This was the shooter. This is

11

where you sat and did your job. If the outhouse had a bench with two holes, it was called a two-holer. If it was a big outhouse it might have three holes, making it a three-holer. There weren't many three-holers in the Utley community. Never heard of a one-holer which really made more sense! Butch often wondered why there were two- or three-holers. Did you really expect that two or three people were going to sit next to each other and take a crap? Doubt it!

Butch hated the two-holer. Like he said, hot in the summer, cold in the winter. Most of the time there wasn't any toilet paper. Toilet paper costs money. What was used instead of toilet paper was an old J.C. Penney or Sears & Roebuck catalog. Sears was called Sears & Roebuck back then. Never knew what happened to Roebuck! Just tear out the page and wipe on page five hundred two. Good ole catalogs. They were used for more than just reading and ordering merchandise.

Just to prepare to go to the toilet was a major production. Butch was sitting in the house listening to the *Lone Ranger and Tonto* on the radio when the urge hit him. It was the big one. He had to poop! It was winter, it was cold, there was snow on the ground, the wind was blowing and he was seven years old.

Butch put on his coat, his hat, gloves, and boots. It was a long way to the outhouse, upwards of sixty feet. There was no light outside the house to show him the way. Armed only with a dim flash light, he was off into the great rotunda. There was snow on the ground, no way to know exactly where the outhouse was. Butch moved slowly in the general direction.

A million thoughts went through Butch's mind when he had to go to the two-holer at night. Thoughts of a boogyman getting him, worse yet, that he might fall in and no one would find him until the next day! He imagined everybody getting up in the dark cold morning, getting ready for breakfast. Butch's dad grabbing the ole Sears & Roebuck and going out to the two- holer. Once inside, he dropped his pants and looks into the hole. Why anyone would look into the hole, maybe he expected to see a snake or whatever? Much to his surprise, there's ole Butch's shit covered face staring up. To Butch this could have really happened!

Butch went inside the two-holer, off with the gloves, unbuttons the coat, takes down the pants. He put the flash light next to him near the second hole. All of a sudden he hears a voice in his ears. It's his dad's voice "DON'T DROP THE LIGHT IN THE HOLE." Butch lifted himself up on the cold hard wood. He was so cold his little butt was turning blue. He grunts for all he's worth. Nothing. Pulling up his pants, he buttons his coat, puts on the gloves and, oh yes, picks up the flashlight. Off to the house. Inside Harold, in his ever caring way asks "Everything come out alright?"

*** THE SLUSH BUCKET ***

There was an answer to the nightly trip to the outhouse, however. It was the SLUSH BUCKET. The slush bucket was a pail about ten to twelve inches round and about twelve high and had a lid on it. If you had money it was made of porcelain. If you didn't have

14

money it was made of metal covered with porcelain. It was the answer to the poor man's inside toilet. However, you only used the slush bucket at night or when you were sick and could not go to the two-holer. You only peed in the slush bucket, NEVER POOPED! Can you imagine what the slush bucket smelled like when you were the third or fourth person to use it? It would make your eyes run, your ears curl and all you really wanted to do now is throw up in the bucket. The next day the woman of the house would take the slush bucket to empty in the outhouse.

Ole Butch just couldn't deal with the outhouse anytime, let alone at night in the dark in the cold. If he had to go, he did IT in the slush bucket. Next person to use the slush bucket got a good whiff of Butch's deposit. Next morning when Ma Vaughn emptied the bucket, she hollered, "HAROLD, BUTCH CRAPPED IN THE THE BUCKET AGAIN!!"

*** THE TUB ***

Take a bath? Well sure. Butch didn't have a shower or a bathtub. What Butch did have was a galvanized metal tub about three feet in diameter and about eighteen high. Once a week, usually on Saturday, the tub was set in the middle of the kitchen. Ma Vaughn would fill it half full with cold water, as they had no running hot water, then add hot water that she heated on the kitchen stove, which is why the tub was in the kitchen. The heat from the kitchen stove also provided heat for the room you were bathing in. Not much privacy. Anyone could see ole Butch taking his bath. In between tub baths he just took little birdie baths, washing his arms, face, hands, feet, what he could without having to get into the tub.

Butch doesn't remember ever seeing his mother or dad, or for that matter, his older brother Jack ever take a bath in the tub. They must have though. Ya think?

The tub never really got warm. Butch would just shiver and shake. His fingers would wrinkle. Butch said when he got out of the tub and looked down he would have to look twice to tell if he was a boy or a girl.

CHAPTER FOUR

*** SCHOOL TIME, SCHOOL TIME ***

Butch was four years old when he started school. He was small for his age, with light brown hair that looked like it was never combed, blue eyes, with freckles over the bridge of his nose and under both eyes, something like a raccoon. His clothes were almost always dirty, no matter how hard his mother tried to keep him clean. His shoes were always untied.

In the part of the neighborhood Butch was raised, most of the kids were older than him. Butch's older brother's friends would come over and visit. While they were there they would teach Butch to swear, and swear Butch did often and loud! Butch knew every dirty, filthy

18

word there was. He could swear like a sailor. Butch often said he could speak two languages, filth and English. He knew filth better. One day when Butch was walking through his neighbor's yard, he stepped in some goat poop. The neighbor raised goats for the milk. The neighbor heard Butch say "dad damn doats." Butch was about three.

Somewhere there's a picture of Butch sitting on a dog house getting a haircut with a cigar in his mouth while his dad was cutting his hair. Jack and some other guys were watching. Butch was about four years old at the time. Starting to get the picture of how Butch was raised? Loving parents, just different.

*** KINDERGARTEN DROP OUT ***

By the fall of 1946 when ole Butch was off to school, he had been told all sorts of stories about school, like how mean the teachers were and how horrible school was. When the first day of school came around, Butch was sure he was going to be beaten to death with a rubber hose. What was he to do? Not many wrinkles in the ole brain yet. But Butch was nobody's dummy, even at four. He had it all figured out. He quit school! Just don't go, that's it. Kindergarten dropout. He knew his mother and dad might not buy into the idea. So what to do? Again a simple answer. Butch lived one short block from the school, straight down Brown Street to the school grounds. Butch's mother wanted to walk him to school the first few days. Butch said he didn't need anyone to take him to school so his mother would go to the corner and watch Butch head off to school. When he would reach the school grounds his mother would turn around and go back to the house. Butch would look back and when he saw his mother leave, he was off. A sharp right turn and two or three hundred feet and he was at the railroad trestle. The trestle supported the railroad track that crossed the road near

20

the school. Butch would climb up among the pillars and support beams and hunker down and wait for school to let out. Kindergarten only lasted a half day, a short half day.

Butch didn't have a watch to know when kindergarten let out so he could go home. It didn't matter, he couldn't tell time anyway. Butch had that covered too. He didn't need a watch. Butch could tell when it was time to go to school by the ringing of the bell. He knew when the bell rang the first time it was time to head to the trestle, when the bell rang the second time it was time for him to head home. What a plan! It worked about four or five days. Butch didn't think that the school would miss him, but sure enough the school secretary called home to see what was the matter with him.

The call went something like this, "Mrs. Vaughn, is Butch sick?" Butch's mother, "What do you mean sick?" "Butch hasn't been at school since the first day."

When Butch got home his mother asked "How did school go?" Butch's reply "Okay." Things became very UN-OKAY. You see, his father, Harold, was president of the school board. It just didn't look right for the president of the school board's son to quit school in the kindergarten. Butch's ma, dad, and Jack, along with everyone in the neighborhood had a real laugh. At the time Butch didn't laugh so hard. A close watch was kept on him. Harold asked one day shortly after Butch decided to go back to school, "What did you do in school?" Butch responded, "Looked at the girls' pink panties, drank milk, and slept on a rug."

Well, that's kind of the way it went for Butch in school from then on. He really didn't like school or homework much. By the time third grade rolled around, they started teaching spelling and English, which was his second language. Remember, filth was primary!

Butch didn't really buy into school, so they flunked him! Oh really, they made him take the third grade over? Today they would find some reason to move him on or the parents would get a lawyer and sue the school. Not back then. You can't cut it, you do it over. It must have been an embarrassment to the family. Harold was president of the school board and Jack a top student. Harold was asked if he wanted them to 'condition' Butch to fourth grade. 'Condition' met passing to the next grade to see if you can cut it, and if after a short time you didn't make passing grades, back you go. Harold said no, Butch should repeat third grade. Good call dad! Butch says to this day it was the best

thing that could have happened at that time. Most kids start at age five

and obviously this is when Butch should have started. He really was

where he belonged in the first place. Along with a little persuasion from

his father, 1940s style, Butch buckled down and got passing or better

grades from then on.

CHAPTER FIVE

*** THE GREAT DEPRESSION ***

Yes, that good old Depression. Unemployment sky high, no unemployment insurance, banks closed, no government bailouts for anyone. There wasn't much welfare, but there were soup lines you could stand in and get food and also receive some used clothing. People would live with relatives and in empty houses. Harold and Edna wound up in the Saginaw and Bay City area in Michigan about thirty miles north of Flint.

Harold found a job shoveling sugar beets. They grow underground. The size of the beet is about twice the size of a soft ball in diameter and weighs two and a half to three pounds each. Harold used an iron fork to shovel the beets. The fork had five prongs about eighteen inches long and half an inch around. On the ends of each prong was a round metal ball that prevented the fork from piercing the beet. The fork was so heavy that Edna couldn't even lift it. Harold was five feet five and one hundred forty pounds and shoveled beets ten hours a day, six days a week.

Harold, Edna, and Jack's living quarters was a tent. Edna never got over that summer and fall. It is just the way you look at things. Today we call living in a tent during the summer camping out. We even pay to do it. I guess if you 'have' to live in a tent it's different.

Summer turned into fall, and winter was around the corner. With a couple of dollars in his pocket, Harold and family moved back to Flint. Harold got a much better job at Long Lumber and Coal Company. Now Harold shoveled coal ten hours a day, six days a week. He shoveled the coal onto a truck, drove the truck to private homes, and shoveled the coal into their basements for heat.

Now Sunday was a different story. Harold drove across town to A.C. Spark Plug, his second job shoveling coal. The coal came in by railroad car. The railroad track had not yet been completed due to harsh weather. The coal would be dumped at the end of the track forming a pile of coal that looked like a small mountain. Harold's job was to shovel the coal by hand into his truck and deliver it to the furnace holding area some distance away.

After a winter of shoveling coal, Harold got a job driving an eighteen wheeler. He drove from Midland, Michigan to Pittsburgh,

Pennsylvania. He was on the road five or six days at a time. It wasn't good on the family.

It was 1941, World War II was underway and employment was opening up a little. The shops were hiring and Harold was back in the machine shop business. Nothing better for a depression than a good old war.

CHAPTER SIX

*** BUILDING THE SHOP ***

In 1949 Butch's dad thought it was about time to start his own machine shop business. All he needed was a building, the machines and money. By the way, Harold didn't have any business experience. Outside of that, Harold was ready to go. No big deal for a guy that only went through the tenth grade. This guy had some big ones, didn't he?

Harold decided that he and Jack would build the machine shop next to the house. You probably could not build a machine shop today as they did in those days. You would have to have a building permit, get an electrical wiring permit, hire a licensed electrician, get the property rezoned light industrial. No, they just built it.

The 'shop', as it was to be known, was a building the size of a two car garage, made from cement block, built on a cement slab. No problem, right? Oh yeah, money. Harold didn't have any. Well, just go to the bank and they will lend you all you need. No, you have to have collateral. Harold used to say if you had all the collateral you needed you probably didn't need the loan. The only collateral Harold had was

27

the house that he and Edna owned. Putting up the house for the loan didn't make Edna very happy. Edna didn't know much about machine shop business or any other business. With some of the extra money Harold borrowed from the bank, he bought a few used machines, a lathe, mill, grinder, etc. and moved them into the shop.

Harold's first business came from owners of small machine shops that he had worked in as an employee. Subcontracting from machine shops that subcontract from larger machine shops won't make you rich, but it will get you started.

The world of business, bidding on jobs, was something that Harold never learned to do. He just knew how to do the machining and was very good at that. Most of the men that Harold contracted from took advantage of his lack of business savvy. They would get a contract with a large company like GM and take the meat, most of the money, and throw Harold the bone. He would say, "After a while you could see the knife coming, you just had to look over your shoulder." Harold worked a regular job during the day and taught Jack the business in the evenings.

Jack was very bright and picked up on the trade quickly. Harold

was getting more and more jobs. Things were looking up, life was

getting better.

CHAPTER SEVEN

*** HERE WE GO AGAIN ***

While Harold was working, doing all that shoveling sugar beets and coal, driving truck on the road, not eating well or often, he got a double hernia and a bad stomach. Harold developed ulcers of the stomach. Of course he took care of it right away. Right? No, he didn't feel he could take time off work. There wasn't any sick pay, no government health insurance, and not very good hospitalization. Harold's stomach got so bad he was eating soda crackers in milk and baby food. He was still working over eight hours during the day and two to three hours at night and every Saturday and Sunday. Holidays became another work day and there weren't any vacations.

The ulcers got so bad they had to operate. This was a very serious and dangerous operation in 1952. They had to cut Harold from the very top of his stomach to as far down as they could go to have a good look at everything. If they would have cut any lower they could have given him the first vasectomy.

First, the doctors had to cut a hole in his stomach and put in a drain tube. No big deal today, but back in 1952 it was a very big deal.

In the 1950s there wasn't any sick pay. There were food banks you could get peanut butter and a few other commodities. There was no money to pay house payments, no money to pay light or heat bills, no one to pay the hospital bills that insurance didn't cover. You went into the hospital a week or so, and went home to recuperate a week or two, and then went back to work. The only money Harold had was what little he and Edna saved in the cookie jar.

Harold weighed less than one hundred forty pounds when he went back to work. Did I forget to tell you that he had a double hernia operation a few years before, thanks to all that shoveling he did?

After a while work picked up and Harold decided that he would quit working for others and start full time with Jack. This guy, Harold, had some big ones, real big brass ones!

CHAPTER EIGHT

*** THE SHOP ***

The 'shop' didn't really have a name. One day when Harold was running a lathe and the chips of metal were curling out on the floor, someone said "Harold why don't you call the shop Blue Chip?" The metal chips were so hot, and mixed with the cutting oil he was putting on the hot metal for cooling, the chips were blue. Thereafter the shop was called Blue Chip Tool & Die. About the same time Harold and Jack were building the machine shop building, Harold decided to build an addition to the house which later became known as...the Utility Room.

*** THE UTILITY ROOM ***

The utility room was attached to the house and was built on a cement slab. Everything seemed to be built on a cement slab. The room was about half the size of the house.

Before the room, Edna would have to fill the washing machine with cold water and add hot water that she heated on the cooking stove.

To keep the water warm she would have to put a little heating device into the wash machine. It's a wonder that device didn't burn the house down. This heater was made of metal, about six inches long, four inches wide, two inches thick, with twenty-five or thirty little holes in it to let the water heat and bubble. Edna would plug this into a socket in the wall. Very dangerous. Ah, but now hot water.

Guess what else the utility room contained? A shower, yes a real shower! Well, sort of a shower. The shower was a painted sheet metal box about three feet square and six or seven feet tall. There was a hot and cold water shower head and it worked great! Best of all, the utility room had a shooter, a toilet, no more runs in the dark, in the cold, to take a crap. You even got to use real toilet paper. What next? Life was great.

The first person to use the new shooter was Harold. He was off to do what men have been doing for centuries, take a crap. What happened next is true, I kid you not. A few minutes later Harold hollers out, "Come here, come here!" Oh no! Edna and Butch thought. The shooter is shot, it fell apart, it's broken beyond repair. They rushed into the utility room over to where the shooter was and there stood Harold, pants up but unbuckled, staring down with a very somber look on his face looking into the shooter. Harold pointed, Edna and Butch looked. And there it was, THE TURD, Butch could never have imagined! Butch being only ten, and not a connoisseur of turds, was not sure if it was a world's record, but it sure was big! You see back in the day of the two-holer you really couldn't get a good perspective for the magnitude of a turd, the hole was so dark and so deep.

CHAPTER NINE

*** ONE OF THE BOYS ***

Butch was making real strides in social development. He was becoming one of the boys, part of the small clique. To accomplish this in the Utley community in the late forties, early fifties you had to be big and strong or little and mean. Butch wasn't big, so little and mean it was. Him and some of the boys, all a little older, would go down to that same railroad trestle Butch went to when he quit school in the kindergarten, but this time for a different reason: to smoke, swear, tell dirty jokes, and lie. Butch was among the best. No one could swear, smoke, curse, or lie like Butch.

CHAPTER TEN

*** SEX EDUCATION 101 ***

Remember what Butch liked most in kindergarten? The girls' in pink panties. That really hadn't changed much by the time he was ten. As a matter of fact, he became more interested in girls and was ready to learn more. Wouldn't you know it, right down Pound Drive just one hundred yards away, there was Beverly ready and willing to help in Butch's education. Sex education 101. Home schooling at its best.

Beverly was the first older woman in Butch's life. She was thirteen, closer to fourteen, and just starting to blossom out, if you know what I mean.

Beverly was a very average looking girl, a little on the skinny side. She was what Butch called hornier than a three-peckered billy goat. Beverly liked boys, all boys, and all the boys liked her.

Butch knew there was a difference between boys and girls. He just wasn't sure what the difference really was. After going to the shed out back of Beverly's house two or three times a week, he found out. That is where the magic happened.

36

On Butch's first trip to 'the shed', as it became known, Beverly didn't say much. She just undressed herself and stood there. Butch just looked her over real good, starting from her head on down. Everything seemed to be the same, a little more development in the breast area, but not so much different. Past the waist, oh, now there was something different, or a lack of something! So this is what little girls are made of.

After that a little touchy here, a little feely there. That was kind of fun. Not as much as baseball, but kind of fun. Not real sex, but as close to it as a ten year old boy and a thirteen year old girl could come to sex in the early 1950s. Butch said it was like a dog trying to catch a car, car stops, dog stops and looks around wondering what to do next. Butch was the dog, Beverly was the car.

CHAPTER ELEVEN

*** THE MOVE ***

Ah, life is really good now. It's summer, no school. Boys down to the trestle, cursing, lying, telling dirty jokes, smoking, and of course, Beverly. What could be better than that?

Then one night at the dinner table where everything of any importance was talked about, Harold made the big announcement, "We're moving." Butch asked, "What the hell you talking about? Move why, where, when?" The only thing Butch is thinking about is "Can we take Beverly?" Why move from this wonderful neighborhood? Muddy streets, hot and cold school rooms with sub-par teachers, getting into fights and losing most of them. What do you mean leave?

It appears that the neighbor next door complained to the electric company that the machines were making his TV act up. The only thing you could do to a TV back then was improve it. All you had was an antenna on the roof and one station in Flint, and that didn't come in clear. The very same neighbor next door used to do arc welding in the evenings which really did interfere with TV reception. Harold's shop did not.

Business was growing and Harold was buying more machinery and needed more space. Time to move. Harold had worked with a couple of guys in Fenton, and when he mentioned moving they suggested a small town they lived in. The town was Byron. Byron was twenty-five or thirty miles from the Utley community, about a million miles away culturally.

Byron's population back then was six hundred people, cats and dogs included, and was ninety-nine percent farmland. Today Byron's population is about six hundred people, cats and dogs included, and is mainly farmland. Byron hasn't changed much. The business district consists of buildings only two stories high. The main street, which is Saginaw Street, is two blocks long. The Shiawassee River runs behind the business district. There's a mill pond behind the school and adjacent to the cemetery. The mill pond is a small lake about four or five feet deep for the most part and maybe a quarter of a mile in diameter. In Byron you fish, hunt, go to school, work on a farm. Everybody goes to church on Sunday. That's it, a real Tom Sawyer- Huckleberry Finn kind of place.

Butch says most of the kids in Byron in the 1950s wouldn't say "shit" if they had a mouth full of it. And as for any Beverlys, forget it. The girls in Byron must have been told if they hold hands or kiss a boy, their tits would fall off. Butch said they all must have held hands or kissed someone, as for the most part, the girls didn't need a bra, all they needed was a band- aid.

Butch's family lived in an apartment above the shop. Most of the businesses in Byron had apartments upstairs. The business owners either lived in or rented the apartments. Harold had purchased a double building. There were two businesses side by side. They shared a common wall. Each building was twenty-four feet wide and forty feet long and made of brick, very old buildings, as all the business buildings were in Byron. Butch and his parents lived in the north side of the building that faced Saginaw Street. The living room area had a big picture window that overlooked the entire two block area of downtown Byron. You could see it all, even the blinker light at the main four corners of town. No traffic light, just a stop sign and blinker light.

Byron wasn't big enough for a real traffic light.

The apartment itself was, well, let's say it was a dump. A real dump! A rat hole if you will! There were mice everywhere. Butch had to sleep on the couch until the apartment was complete. Almost every night he would be awakened by a mouse crawling on him.

Butch had to write a small essay in the fifth grade. The essay was about the mice in his house. Butch said that his mother would trap the mice and cook them to eat and freeze their tails to be used as toothpicks. The teacher thought that was quite creative and gave Butch a passing grade. Little did she know how many mice there really were.

The apartment hadn't been lived in for years. There was just one long wall through the length of the apartment and it sagged. Butch's dad was a hard worker and all around handyman. Harold was able to fix up the apartment quite well. He portioned off rooms into a kitchen, two bedrooms, and, oh yes, a real bathroom with a bathtub that stood up on four short feet. The tub was already there when Butch and family arrived. The main floor was mainly empty. It had been used as a restaurant a few years back. Harold had to shore up the main floors on both sides to support the machinery. He built cement block pillars in

41

the basement and poured cement on the shop floors. It worked just fine. As a matter of fact, it was the only building in Byron that the Civil Defense would certify as a bomb shelter.

Yes, we had bomb shelters back then. On the front door of the new shop building was the black and yellow sign signifying that this building was a bomb shelter and that there were survival supplies in the basement. Civil Defense put several containers in the basement. The containers were to be filled with water. There were also several boxes of C and K rations in the basement as well. They stayed there for years after Civil Defense closed bomb shelters.

The second building which shared a common wall was the south side. The building blocked the view of the family next door from seeing the business district. All they could see was the old two story red brick building.

In the south building Harold also built an apartment. That apartment became home for Jack and his wife and later for Butch and his wife. On the main floor of the south side was the remains of what in former years was a mortuary. At the back end of the building in a corner were the former tenant's stored coffins. This is where Harold built shelving for tool and dies to be stored. He would call it coffin corner. When Harold needed something from that area he would say, "Go and get this or that from coffin corner." Everybody knew where he meant.

Harold also found a plate that was used to put on a coffin. It read 'rest in peace'. He put that on the shop bathroom door.

CHAPTER TWELVE

*** THE FIGHT THAT NEVER HAPPENED ***

The first few days in Byron was really tough on Butch. He had

to get up the nerve to go out the door, down the stairs, and walk

downtown. Butch was the new kid on the block. He knew when a new

kid moved into the Utley community and started walking around he

would have to fight his way home just to show where he stood. Win or

lose it didn't matter. Like it or not it was time for Byron's new kid to

make the walk. There would be no knives, clubs, guns, just a short

thumping. That was the Utley way. On with the T-shirt, blue jeans, and

tennis shoes. Out the door, down Saginaw Street, ass kicked or not,

Byron here we come.

Oh no! There he was, a full head taller and much heavier than Butch. Remember Butch isn't very big, just mean. He didn't win many of his fights at Utley, but always put up a good one. No matter, it still hurts. All of a sudden this kid comes at him with a smirk on his face and he sticks out his hand and says "Hi, I'm David." At first Butch looked at him and thought this was some kind of trick they pull in Byron. But slowly Butch shook David's hand and said, "I'm Butch."

David had a grip like a vice. Butch was sure glad David didn't want to fight. Dave would have killed him. Come to find out Dave was going to be in fifth grade, same as Butch.

Dave asked, "Hey Butch, if you want to play some baseball we'll be down at the field around two." Dave pointed in the direction of the baseball field. How great was that! Butch wasn't big, but he sure could play baseball.

Just then something crawled around Dave's neck and Butch jumped back. "What the hell is that?"

Dave laughed and said, "That's my pet raccoon. I have some pigeons at home, too."

Butch thought, "So there really is a Tom Sawyer."

45

As Dave turned around and started walking away, the raccoon took a crap right down Dave's back! Dave picked up the raccoon and says, "Oh shit!"

"Well," Butch thought, "they call it the same here as at Utley except at Utley they don't wear it, it's just a figure of speech."

CHAPTER THIRTEEN

*** IT'S IN A BROWN BOTT LE ***

Sometime after Butch met David, he got acquainted with some of the other guys. One of them was Del. One afternoon Butch and Del went down in the basement of the shop where they used to do the embalming when it was a mortuary. They were just looking around when they came across some brown bottles that had not been opened. The light wasn't very good in the basement. What the boys thought they discovered was some beer. "Del, there must be a dozen bottles here, better than Pike's wine." Butch was referring to Doc Pike, the old veterinarian, who was a wino. Doc Pike would hide his wine stashes in the alley behind the Byron Hardware, under the stairs leading to one of

47

the apartments. Butch and Del would steal a snort or two every once in awhile. Just as Butch was about to open and take a drink, Del noticed that it said formaldehyde on the bottle. Butch and Del almost got pickled in more ways than one!

CHAPTER FOURTEEN

1957-58

*** TOM SAWYER AND HUCK FINN ***

Another new friend that Butch met was Skeeter. Butch was

Tom Sawyer, Skeeter was Huck Finn. Skeeter was about fourteen years

old, average in height for his age, quite thin, with dusty brown hair and

blue eyes. Most of the time Skeeter had a big smile on his face.

Skeeter came from a very large family that was quite poor. His father

had been put in the state mental hospital in Pontiac. Skeeter's mother

was now living with her seven children in what they called a common

law marriage. Her common law husband's name was Vernon, referred

to as Vern. If you lived with someone for a length of time you were

considered in a common law marriage. At least that was what

everybody said. Who knows if it really was the law or not. Today

we just say significant other and let it go at that. There weren't many

common law arrangements back then and they were not looked upon

favorably.

Skeeter, his mother, Vern, the significant other, and seven

brothers and sisters lived in a small but well-kept wood frame house on

the bank of the Shiawassee River.

Then there was Old Vern, yep old Vern, Vern's dad. It really

doesn't take much to keep up with the family tree in Byron! Old Vern

lived in a small one room wooden structure, about the size of a large

living room. The house if you wanted to call it a house, set back from

the road about two hundred feet, resting almost in the Shiawassee River.

There were several trees in front of the house, so you really couldn't

see the house from the road.

The house had a wood floor, one wooden door in the front and

one wooden door in the rear. Both doors had a rope through a hole in

the door where most doors had a door knob. The rope had a knot in

each end that you pulled to open or close the door. There were two

small windows on each side of the front door. You could hardly see

50

through them, they were always dirty. The windows were never opened. When the heat got so bad in the summer, old Vern would just open both doors to get a breeze. The house was lit by one sixty watt bulb hanging by a cord over an old wooden table in the center of the room. The house was furnished with a wooden kitchen table and four wooden chairs and a broken down bed. The only other light old Vern had was a kerosene lamp that he could carry around for light whenever he needed it.

On the back wall were some makeshift cupboards that old Vern used for the few dishes that he had. The cupboards were just a wood frame box with one shelf in the middle. No doors. Just under the cupboards was a chipped old enameled sink with a hand pump to pump water for cooking, washing dishes, etc. No running water, no hot water, no bathroom. He had not caught up with the rest of Byron that had hot and cold running water and a bathroom. He still had to use the old two-holer out back.

Old Vern himself was quite a piece of work. He stood about five feet six inches and weighed maybe one hundred fifteen pounds. He had a bald head except for a small strip of hair that ran along the back of his head from one side to the other. You never really saw his bald head as he always wore a worn out fedora. Old Vern didn't have a tooth in his head. His mouth and cheeks were sunk in, eyes deep set in their sockets.

Butch didn't know much about living or dying at this stage of his life, but he knew one thing. Old Vern looked like death eating a cracker.

Butch and Skeeter would go to old Vern's shack, the name they gave for old Vern's house. Butch and Skeeter would have talks. Talks about girls, money, and girls. Old Vern didn't say much but seemed to like to have the boys around. He would even smile once in a while and nod his head. He just liked to listen to the two boys talk about what they were doing and what plans they had for the future.

Old Vern looked like a guy whose time had passed and was waiting to die, which he did a short time after Butch first met him.

The only people at old Vern's funeral was young Vern, Skeeter's mother, Skeeter, Butch, and Skeeter's seven brothers and sisters. Skeeter and Butch were the only two to shed a tear. Who really cares about an old worn out man like old Vern? Who cares about what an old man thinks? Apparently, only Tom Sawyer (Butch) and

Huck Finn (Skeeter). Butch often wondered what old Vern thought and

dreamed about when he was a young man. I hope I grow up to be an

old bald headed man, with no teeth, living in a shack on the bank of the

Shiawassee River. Maybe not.

A few days after they buried old Vern, they burned his shack

down and everything in it.

During many of the conversations held at old Vern's shack,

Skeeter and Butch talked about making money. There wasn't much a

twelve year old could do to make a buck in Byron, there wasn't a

McDonald's, there was only a paper route. Kids used to deliver

newspapers door to door back then, and there was only one paper route.

There was always bailing hay and other farm related work. Skeeter was

fourteen or so, old enough to work on a farm, but not very strong, and

Butch was only twelve and small. There had to be another way.

CHAPTER FIFTEEN

*** RATS ***

Rats, that's what we'll do, rats. Lots of money in rats. Don't cost much to get into the rat business. Couple of traps, that's all.

The rats Skeeter was referring to were muskrats. Muskrat fur, fox, mink and other furry animals were used for years to make ladies' fur coats. A muskrat, for you who may not know, is just that, a rat, a rodent. It has beady little black eyes, and it's teeth in front are very narrow and long, and yellow. It is about as long as your common sewer rat, but about twice the weight.

The muskrats that Skeeter and Butch were going to trap lived along the banks of the Shiawassee River and on the banks of the Byron Mill Pond. The rats dig a hole in the side of the bank or just under the

54

water next to the bank and then dig a hole up so they are hidden and dry.

Skeeter, being the outdoors guy, fishing, hunting, etc. knew all you needed to know about trapping. Well, he knew more than Butch. Skeeter said he would teach Butch all he needed to know. With Skeeter's brains and Butch's money to buy the traps, they were in business. Actually, Skeeter and Butch had no money. However, Butch's dad did have some money and somehow Butch convinced his dad to back the S & B Muskrat business. Butch doesn't know if his dad thought it would be a good learning experience in the world of work and business or if he thought they were both nuts and wanted to see how it would play out. Butch thinks it was a little of both.

Off to buy the traps. The boys bought sixteen traps. Why sixteen traps, nobody knows! Maybe that's how much money Butch's dad gave him.

A muskrat trap or small animal trap, the kind used by the boys, looked just like the kind you see in the movies or on television. The small animal traps they used didn't have the teeth in the jaws of the trap. The jaws were smooth, just two steel jaws that slammed together holding the little critter until you got there to release them.

Next, Skeeter showed Butch how to set the trap. All you do is push down on the handle of the trap with your foot. That opens the two jaws and you set the latch in the middle. It's just like setting a mouse trap. Don't let your finger get caught or you'll come up with a stub.

Skeeter explained, "Well Butch, now you know how to set the trap, you'll need to know where to set them. We'll go along the banks of the mill pond up behind the cemetery and look for holes in the bank where rats go in and out. We'll set the traps just at the entrance to the rat hole, cover the trap with leaves so the ole rat won't see it and when the rat leaves the water to enter his home, slam! Bang! goes the trap and we got the sucker, got him by the foot. When we check the traps to see if we get anything, we may just find all we have is a foot."

"A foot? What about the rat?" Butch asked.

"Well if he's in the trap for some time he will gnaw off his foot to get out. We're left with a foot and Mister Muskrat is left with three. There's been many a time I would get a rat with only three feet.

"When we check the traps and there is a rat in the trip, the next thing is getting him out. The rat is not going to be real happy at this point. He's pissed off. You can't just reach down and pick the rat up and put him in your bag. That's a good way to lose a finger and the better part of your hand. You have to kill him first and then get him out of the trap," Skeeter told him.

"Kill em how?"

"Smack 'em in the head with a baseball bat or ax handle. That's the way most do it. What's bad about that is you might not kill the rat, you may just stun them or knock them out for a bit. Then when you reach down to get them out of the trap they wake up. You think they were pissed off before, now they're really pissed. You slammed their foot in a trap, put a goose egg on their head and all they got on their mind is getting the hell out of there and the best way is to bite the living crap out of you. What we're going to use is this."

Skeeter pulled out a toy looking rifle. It was a twenty-two caliber rifle that shoots twenty-two caliber shorts. A twenty-two caliber short, refers to the size of bullet it shoots, a twenty-two short being about the smallest rifle there is. It was used a lot in Butch's time for hunting squirrel, rabbit, groundhog, and all kinds and size of varmints. This twenty-two looked homemade, and was about two feet long with an unfinished, unpainted wooden stock that was about one inch thick and had a sawed off twenty-two bolt action barrel screwed on.

Skeeter said, "This is just the ticket, small, light and deadly. Just put the barrel close to the rat's head and shoot him right between the lookers, Bam! Dead rat!

"We'll split the run. I'll run in the morning and you run in the afternoon. Next you run in the morning and I'll run in the afternoon. You run the line twice a day so they're not left in the trap for a long period of time and start that gnawed foot routine."

Skeeter stated, "We'll split the money fifty-fifty. We'll take the rats out to ole Ned and get fifty cents apiece ungutted. We might even trap a mink, who knows. Mink will bring ten or fifteen dollar a piece."

Ned was a live bait and fur buyer at Myers Lake. Ned sold minnows, worms, and grubs, to fishermen and bought and sold hides. Ned would pay fifty cents for an animal that was not skinned, a little more if you gutted and skinned them. You really needed to know what you were doing if you planned to gut and skin rats, mink, and the such. If you didn't do it just right, the pelt or fur would be worth less money so most young trappers sold the trapped animals whole. Ned would sometimes say the rat was too small or the fur was damaged and would pay only a quarter.

The real drawback to trapping wasn't killing or running the line. It was more when and where you trapped. You have to run the trap line early in the morning when they're leaving and early in the evening when they're returning. You trap for muskrats in the winter. This meant getting up early, really early, before school, in the dark, in the cold. Temperature was usually in the teens if not lower, and after dinner in the cold, in the dark.

Oh, by the way, do you remember where we set the traps? On the banks of the mill pond around THE CEMETERY. Picture it again in the cold, in the dark, in the CEMETERY. All kinds of thoughts can go through the mind of a thirteen year old. After about three weeks of this, Butch retired from the muskrat business, dissolved the S& B fur business, and let Skeeter have all the traps. Thus the end of Butch's first adventure in the wide world of business. Butch didn't see much of Skeeter after that.

Skeeter's life wasn't very normal, whatever normal is. He had a lot of jobs, mainly in construction, hung out in bars, married, had several kids in his adult life. Skeeter's wife died when Skeeter was

in his sixties. Skeeter didn't have much to do after that but drink. The

last two things Skeeter did as an adult was rape his grandniece, his

brother's son's daughter who was twenty years old. Skeeter was sixty-

eight years old. Sixty eight! You don't know whether to pat him on the

back for having the strength to do it or hang him from the tallest tree.

Skeeter took care of the problem by putting a gun in his mouth and

blowing off the top of his head. This is the end of Skeeter (Huck Finn).

CHAPTER SIXTEEN

*** DISABILITY ***

Life goes on. Well, for some anyway.

When Skeeter and Butch were in the rat business, Skeeter introduced Butch to a guy named Darold. Darold was a lot older than Butch or Skeeter. He was about twenty or twenty one. Darold was very small in stature, maybe five foot three and less than one hundred twenty pounds.

What was unique about Darold is he didn't have fingers on either hand or toes on either foot. All the guys called him Stub. Not very nice, but the name Stub really didn't seem to bother Darold. Stub had an operation on his hands when he was young. The doctors made incisions on both hands where the thumb and index finger would be.

61

Apparently there was enough of what was needed to allow the doctor to make what would work like fingers. Butch was always amazed at the things Stub could do. Stub could zip and unzip his pants to pee and poop and wipe his butt. Butch thought that was quite an accomplishment.

Stub could do most things. He could even bait a fish hook. People with two goods hands have a hard time doing that.

One day Butch was over to Stub's house. He lived with his mother. Butch said something like "Stub, it's time to go." At that moment Stub's mother shouted out, "What did you say?" Butch being dumbfounded said, "What?" Stub chimed in and said, "My ma don't like people calling me Stub."

Butch listened for a good two minutes while Darold's mother gave him the what for. Butch never really meant any disrespect to Darold when he called him Stub. Butch just used it as a nickname, like people calling him Butch. You can bet on one thing, after Darold's mother chewed Butch out, Butch never called Stub "Stub" in front of Darold's mother anymore. From that day on when anyone else called him Stub, Butch corrected them by saying, "His name is Darold."

Life isn't always fair. Sometimes your biggest accomplishment is just zipping and unzipping your pants. That can mean more than making a million.

Years later, Butch wondered what would have happened if he would have asked his dad to consider hiring Darold. Butch's dad was very receptive to hiring people with disabilities. Harold once hired a man who lost his right arm in a farming accident. The man worked out quite well. After a few years he moved on to a better paying job.

Butch lost contact with Darold and doesn't know what happened to him and hopes that life was good to him.

This was Butch's first lesson in being sensitive to other people, be it a physical or mental condition, religion, color of skin or nationality. Believe me, there was going to be plenty of issues of prejudices in Butch's life. Remember this was just the middle 1950s. Look out 60s.

CHAPTER SEVENTEEN

*** BEST FRIEND ***

Tom was Butch's best friend when Butch was fifteen. Tom was what you might call a man's man, rough and ready. Tom never picked a fight, but he sure, never ran from one. He always seemed to be where one was. Butch said you could kill Tom by hitting him in the head but you could never hurt him.

Tom was about five feet nine or so and weighed one seventy-five. He had wavy light brown hair, blue eyes, nice looking, loved to fight. A two hundred pounder could hit him but not hurt him.

Tom had three brothers Gary, Phil and Nick. Tom, Gary and Nick were built just like their dad, short, stocky, and tough as nails. They all became bald as adults. Phil was taller and thin, but just as mean.

Tom's dad moved up from Missouri with his mother. He worked at GM and bought a small farm. He always tried to teach the boys how to farm and farm correctly. Tom's dad told him how he wanted a field plowed. Tom wasn't plowing quite the way his father wanted, so his dad explained it to him the best way he knew how.

His dad climbed up on the tractor and leaned over very gently and smacked him right alongside the head, knocking him off the tractor. His dad never had to explain plowing to him again.

Tom's dad caught him smoking. His dad didn't want his sons to smoke. He felt he had to discipline Tom in the same way he did with the tractor. He was not going to smack Tom in the head for smoking. Oh no. He simply asked Tom how many cigarettes he had left in his pack. Tom said, "Three." His dad said, "Take them out of the pack and put them in your mouth, chew them up and swallow them." Tom did just that, remembering the incident on the tractor. First, he choked a little, then he gagged a little, turned red in the face, finally green around the gills. Then he puked, followed by the green-apple two-step diarrhea. Tom was real glad he didn't have a full pack.

Tom and his two brothers, Phil and Gary all joined the military. When all three got home on leave there was sure to be trouble.

It was a Saturday night, the boys were in a bar drinking and a fight broke out. Go figure! The fight went outside and Tom was knocked down. The other guy jumped up and down on Tom's leg and broke it in two places. One break was just below the knee and the other above the ankle.

Butch said to Tom, "That wasn't very fair of that guy to jump up and down on your leg when you were down."

Tom said, "Remember the rules of a street fight, there are no rules." Tom was taken to the hospital where he met and fell in love with his nurse.

Tom did straighten out somewhat. While he was recuperating from his broken leg at a military hospital, he and another guy had a difference of opinion and, what do you know, a fight broke out right in the hospital! Tom got a black eye, nose bleed, and a cut lip. The other guy didn't do well either.

Tom married his nurse and had two boys, retired from the military after twenty-one years of service, and came back home and worked fifteen years for GM. Tom is in his early seventies, still married to the same woman. She must have been some woman. They are doing well.

Tom's brother Phil, one of the three boys in the bar fight, turned out okay with just a little drinking problem.

Nick, the youngest brother, had a motorcycle accident and lost his left leg just below the knee. He died a few years later of a heart attack at the age of thirty.

Gary, the third brother, was a little bit stranger than the others. Gary and Tom had been drinking a little too much. Gary was driving. Gary asked Tom what would happen if he put the car in park while they were moving at a speed of fifty-plus miles an hour. Tom said, "I don't know, give it a try." He did. The car rolled over two or three times. Neither one got a scratch. Boys will be boys.

Gary lived in a small town of about five thousand people, married and had five kids. A couple of the kids got involved with drugs. Gary went to the city police, county and state police. He told them who the drug dealer was. The police all said, "Yes, we know who the person is and we're trying to get enough evidence to arrest and prosecute."

Gary was not what you would call a very patient man. He knew the drug dealer hung out in a local watering hole called the 602 Bar. One evening he entered the 602 Bar armed with a twelve gauge shotgun with double ought buck shot. A twelve gauge shotgun with double

67

ought buckshot at close range could blow your head off.

Gary walked over to where the drug dealer was sitting and said, "You SOB" and shot him. It knocked the drug dealer over backwards in his chair. Just like in the movies, Gary walked over to the bar, put the shotgun down and said, "Call the police and give me a beer."

Butch doesn't know if Gary got the beer, but Gary did get arrested and sentenced to life in prison. Gary was in his early fifties at the time of the shooting. After serving four or so years Gary died of a brain tumor. That's what the prison officials said anyway. Who knows what really goes on in a prison.

While Tom was in the military his father was having some emotional trouble. Things just got worse. His dad finally took the easy way out. Yep. He put a shot gun in his mouth and blew the top of his head off.

A lot of that was going on back then.

CHAPTER EIGHTEEN

*** A BASEBALL CAREER CUT SHORT ***

There was another lesson for Butch to learn at this time. One summer Butch, about twelve years of age, was practicing baseball with the boys and the coach, Roy, who was only seventeen or eighteen himself. Roy was batting grounders to the infield.

Playing third base was Butch's friend, Allen, who was a very good ball player. Allen was head and shoulders, talent wise, above any of the other players on Butch's team.

Roy was really slapping the balls down hard to Allen. He was getting all of them. Then all of a sudden, Roy double balled Allen. Roy hit one and then hit another back to Allen real fast before he could look up. Roy was just clowning around trying to get one past Allen. The second ball didn't stay on the ground. It was a line drive. It hit Allen in the face just over his right eye. Allen went down momentarily unconscious. They took him home.

The swelling had become so bad the next day, Allen didn't know what was going on. His parents took him to the local hospital and they had him transferred to the University of Michigan Hospital. There the doctors found a blood clot. They had to perform brain surgery. This was 1955 when not much was known about how to operate on the brain.

Allen survived the operation and after several days in the hospital came home. After a few days Allen's mother called and asked if Butch wanted to come visit him. Butch said sure.

Back in those days they didn't have counseling for young people to prepare them for tragedies or death and such.

When Butch walked into Allen's house and saw Allen partly sitting or partly lying on the couch in the living room, Butch was shocked! There was his good friend, an excellent ballplayer, his head very swollen, no hair on his head, a large scar from one side of his head to the other, barely able to hold his head up, eyes not focusing well. Butch couldn't understand a word Allen was saying. Allen had lost the use of his left arm and left leg.

Butch couldn't sleep that night. How could this happen? If it could happen to Allen, it could happen to anyone. One minute you're fine, the next, who knows? Allen did get it back together somewhat. He got his speech back one hundred percent. He could walk but always had a brace on his left leg. The use of his left hand and arm was ninety percent gone.

No sports for Allen. He loved sports so much. He became the team manager, nice name for water boy, all through junior high and high school. Allen was at every game, handing out the towels to his buddies so they could wipe their face, handing them water to drink, putting the balls in the bag, etc., knowing all the time he could have been as good as any of them, probably better. His buddies knew it too. Later Allen graduated from high school, got married, had two sons and a daughter. His oldest son Allen Jr. was a very good ball player. Allen Sr. drove Jr. quite hard.

Allen Sr. lived until he was about sixty-seven. He had lain in a nursing home for over five years, the last year or so curled up in a ball. Only a few visitors outside of family ever visited him. He died in a nursing home of acute depression and complications. Embarrassingly, Butch never made a visit.

CHAPTER NINETEEN

*** ENTREPRENEUR ***

With the taste of the rat business still in Butch's mouth, making money was still on his mind. Talking with a couple of his buddies, Del and Barry, the topic of money came up. All three thought they needed money. What for, they never said.

There wasn't much to do in Byron even if you had money. None of them had a driver's license or car to get anywhere to make money. They were trapped. The unemployment rate for fourteen and fifteen year old teens in Byron was about one hundred percent. There was always farm work. But Butch was still too small to handle the heavy farm work, although he did pick apples and strawberries.

Butch said one of the hardest jobs he ever had was picking strawberries, all the bending over, sun beating down. You don't get much shade in a strawberry patch and the pay was horrible, eighteen cents a rack! A rack was six quarts, and they had to be fully rounded quarts. When the farmer sold a quart of strawberries, the quart was level. Del was older than Butch and Barry, but he was smaller than most boys his age. Barry was a little bigger but still not ready for the heavy lifting of most farm work.

Butch knew one thing, he wasn't going back into the rat business.

*** CHICKENS ***

Del was the older and smarter of the three. That doesn't say much about the brights of Butch and Barry. Remember Del was the one who, a couple of years earlier, was about to drink a bottle of formaldehyde. Well, at least Del was able to read the label!

All of a sudden Del said we can raise chickens. Butch and Barry asked where he came up with that idea. They were standing in the middle of Del's grandma's chicken coop at the time. I told you that Del was the smarter of the three.

The boys were cleaning the chicken coop to make it into a hut.

Back in the day, a hut was anything or anyplace a few boys could gather to have a sort of club and do whatever boys at that age do, mainly lie, smoke, tell dirty jokes, and curse. A lot like the trestle back at Utley, only no Beverly.

The coop was about eighteen feet long, twelve feet wide, and seven feet high, with a slanted roof front to back, one door and three or four windows in the front with four small window panes in each window.

Del's grandma said they could use the coop if they cleaned it up. This chicken coop hadn't been used in about fifteen years or more and still had a good layer of chicken poop on the floor. Didn't smell too bad until you got down to the second and third layers of poop, then it made your eyes water! It's a wonder there wasn't some kind of disease that would get into the boys' lungs.

Butch and Barry asked Del, "What do we know about the chicken business?"

Del said, "We'll ask my grandma. She will tell us what to do and how to do it."

To picture grandma for you, she was seventy-five plus years

old, quite wrinkled, very small, about five feet tall and weighed about ninety pounds soaking wet. Grandma talked a hundred miles an hour. If you caught every third word, you were lucky.

Del asked his grandma if she would help in the boys' venture and she said yes. All three were quite surprised. Looking back, Butch thinks she just wanted to see what these three idiots were going to do. Grandma told the boys the basics of raising chickens. First, they had to buy the chickens. They could get them at the grain elevator. They would cost about five cents apiece. They could also buy the chicken feed they needed there. Grandma had a couple of chicken feeders and waterers the boys could use.

Grandma told the boys they would have to run an electric cord from the house to the coop and drop down two or three lines inside the coop to put seventy-five watt light bulbs, so that the baby chicks would keep warm. The baby chicks were only a few days old when they got them.

The boys would also have to separate the chicks into small groups, depending on how many they got. Baby chicks die easily, mostly from the cold and disease, and it happens quickly. If one or two get sick they will not spread the disease to all the other chicks, maybe just a few in their group. If one of the chicks gets sick or looks weak, the others will peck at it until it dies. Off to the grain elevator the boys went. They bought fifty baby chicks and the feed that went with them.

Back to the chicken coop, the boys marked out the living areas for the baby chicks. First, they made three separate areas to house the chicks, then the boys put old newspapers on the floor for insulation and easy clean up. Then, they cut up cardboard boxes about twelve inches high and made a circle 5 feet in diameter. The boys then dropped the seventy-fve watt light bulbs over the enclosure to keep the chicks warm.

The boys were in the chicken business. Tyson eat your heart out! After a few weeks of feeding, watering, cleaning up poop, throwing out the dead chicks, Butch built up a real dislike for chickens. Butch kept reminding Del and Barry this may not be much fun, but it sure beats the rat business.

During this time the boys were out launching a nation wide sales campaign to sell the chickens once they were ready. Well, maybe not a nation wide campaign, more like a village wide campaign, asking families, friends, and neighbors to buy their chickens.

Now time for step two. The killing. Yuk! But you have to kill a couple chickens if you want to make some bread. The boys thought it wasn't going to be too bad, could be fun. The boys got a little twisted in their thinking once in a while. They really didn't have a clue what to do.

There stood grandma, all wrinkled, bent slightly forward, old dress with apron, talking a million miles an hour, carrying a hatchet and hollering orders as she walks. This, the day of genocide of the chickens.

"You," she pointed to Del, "go get that tree stump." The stump was about twelve inches in diameter, about a twelve inches tall, and had quite a smooth, flat top. "Put it here," she ordered. *Here* was under a big shade tree in the backyard between the coop and Grandma's house. The grass was a little on the long side which the boys found actually helpful in the process.

"You," Grandma pointed to Barry, "get the first chicken." Barry brought the first chicken.

Grandma instructed, "Hold it by the legs with one hand and by the neck and head with the other. Hold it close to you so it doesn't try to get away."

"You," Grandma pointed to Butch, "take the ax."

"You," Grandma pointed to Barry again, "bring the chicken here," pointing to the stump. "Keep holding the chicken by the feet with one hand and with the other hold the chicken under the lower beak with your middle finger and with your pointer finger, index finger, on top of the head. Pull the feet and head at the same time. That will make the chicken stretch out its head. Then real fast lay its neck on the stump. Butch, you whack it with the ax about midway between the head and the body. Make a strong firm swing. Barry, make sure you're out of the way, but still holding the legs. As soon as Butch makes his swing and the head is off, toss it in the grass and let 'em bleed out."

A lot can go wrong here. Miss altogether, not make a clean cut, then you have a chicken with half a head off, eyes bulging, wings flapping, bleeding and you still have to complete the job. Or better yet, Butch could hack Barry's fingers, hand, leg, or some other part of his anatomy. Where's OSHA when you need them?

Butch got ready with the ax, Del got ready to go get the next chicken. Barry pulled on the legs and head the way Grandma said and, sure enough, the chicken stretched out its head. Down went the chicken on the stump and Butch with a nice firm swing chopped off the head. The chicken immediately started to flap its wings and blood started to flow.

Barry, startled, forgot to toss the chicken in the grass. Instead he just held onto it. Blood everywhere and on everyone.

Grandma hollered, "Toss it you damned fool, toss it." And toss it he did. The chicken started flopping on the ground and ran in a circle. To turn a phrase, "Running around like a chicken with its head cut off".

The boys looked at Grandma and Grandma looked quite disgusted with them. The boys were covered with chicken blood, except Grandma who didn't have a drop on her.

Grandma ordered, "Get over to the water spigot and wash yourselves off. Come back and see if you can get it right.

"How many chickens do you have sold?

One of the boys said, "About twenty."

"All right," said Grandma, "nineteen more to go."

Then we plucked 'em, gutted 'em and we were done. At least Butch was. "We'll do half today and the rest tomorrow," Grandma said.

Del asked, "Why half, why not kill 'em all?"

Grandma answered, "I told you, you kill 'em, you pluck 'em, you gut 'em, and, believe me, you'll be a day doing half. We'll put them in my freezer, then you can deliver them to your customers."

Butch offered, "Grandma, we've been thinking and all the help you've been giving us, maybe you should get some of the profits."

Grandma, looking through squinted eyes, standing slightly bent wrinkled body, took a stance with her hands on her hips. In a seldom used low, slow voice, she said, "I don't want any of your money. I don't want to be any part of what you've done or what you will do. I don't want anyone to know I've had any part of any of this. Do you understand?" Somehow the boys understood completely.

The slaughtering began. Del fetched the chickens, Barry pulled the legs and head. The chicken flopped on the block and Butch whacked off the head. Barry now had the chicken by the legs and tossed it on the grass. The chicken flapped it's wings and ran all over bleeding. The boys had a good laugh. Remember their little minds were twisted. Most boys their age were. Lucky nothing went wrong. Well, not too wrong. An 'oops' here and a 'damn' there and before you knew it, ten dead chickens!

The boys said they were sorry that they got so much blood all over grandma's grass. Grandma just smiled and said, "Well, in a couple of days when you're all done killing 'em, plucking 'em, and gutting 'em, you boys get to mow the lawn. You won't even know there was any blood there." Grandma was looking smarter by the minute.

In the meantime Grandma was getting a galvanized tub, the same kind and size tub that Butch used to take a bath in when he lived on Brown Street in the Utley community. Grandma filled the tub with scalding hot water.

The boys asked, "What's that for Grandma?" She gave them one of those quizzical looks, kind of a what-do-you-mean look? When she looked at the three of them standing there hot, stinking of sweat and chicken blood, she must have been thinking stupid, stupid, stupid. And they don't even know it! Of course the boys thought they were pretty smart. Grandma gave them the coop, showed them what to do and they make all the money. The boys just don't know who's the cat and who's the mouse. Who is playing with who. Grandma is just having fun with them.

Grandma answered, "Remember you kill 'em, pluck 'em, gut 'em. Now this is the plucking part."

"You", Grandma pointed to Butch, "bring over one of those dead chickens. Put it in the water. Let 'er soak a minute or two. Then reach in, pull 'er out, and put' er on that piece of cement there and start pulling out the feathers."

Butch put the chicken in the very hot water, let it soak, and then reached in to pick up the chicken.

Butch yelped, "Damn, that's hot!"

"Quit your swearing, you little baby, and get the chicken out of the water and get plucking. The same goes for you other two," Grandma ordered as she swung her arm toward Del and Barry. "If you're agonna pluck chickens, you're agonna get wet and its agonna be hot."

So it went, put the chicken in the hot water, add hot water from time to time, let 'em soak, pull the chicken out, pluck the feathers. Put the feathers in brown paper bags, let 'em dry, then burn them up in the fire barrel. After what seemed an eternity, the boys were done plucking.

Grandma reminded them, "You boys gotta gut" em." You

thought killing and plucking was something to see, you can only imagine the gutting. Three boys with sharp knives and wet slippery chickens. Yikes!

"Bring 'em over here," Grandma pointed to an old wooden table. Grandma picked up a chicken and put it on the table. "Pay attention, I'm agonna show you just once." Grandma stabbed the chicken near the bung hole and slit it up to the breast bone, spreads the legs, reached in and pulled out a hand full of guts. Grandma picked up the hose from the ground and washed the inside of the chicken.

"There, now you do it," Grandma pointed to Del. In spite of Del's gagging, frowning, and distorting his face he managed to gut the chicken and not cut off any fingers or other body parts. Barry was next. The same gagging, frowning, wincing. Then it was Butch's turn.

Butch is like Jack the Ripper and Mack the Knife rolled into one. Butch looked up for Grandma's approval.

Grandma stated, "Not bad there, Butch. Of course it's rectum looks like shredded wheat and you almost cut off its leg, but all in all you boys did quite a good job. Now do the rest of them."

Butch asked, "What do we do with the guts?" Grandma smiled

and said, "We'll feed some to the cats. It gives 'em a shiny coat and they love the stuff. Also you boys will dig the ground around the flowers and bury the guts. They make good fertilizer too."

"What do we do with the chickens when we're all done?"

"Like I said, we'll put them in the deep freezer until you get them sold. How many you got sold now?

"About twenty."

"How many you got altogether?" Grandma asked.

"About forty."

"You better get knocking on doors and sell the rest. Don't want 'em in my deep freezer forever."

The boys sold all forty chickens and turned a nice profit for three not too bright, not too talented boys! They had one thing on their side. Grandma. Thank God for grandmas.

*** TURTLE SOUP ***

Butch was pushing age fifteen. He had already been in business three or four times. Once with Skeeter in the rat business, once with Del and Barry in the chicken business, and in between Butch caught a few turtles in the mill pond and sold them for turtle soup. The most profitable, least investment, and easy work was the turtle business.

One afternoon Butch overheard his neighbor Mr. Houser saying he liked turtle soup. Butch asked, "If I can catch some turtles, how much would you pay for them?"

Mr. Houser replied, "Sure I'll pay you. The price depends on the size of the turtle."

Off to the mill pond. Butch was in the turtle business. Butch found a nice stick and looked at the water's edge. Aha! A turtle! Butch put the end of the stick at the nose of the turtle. The turtle snapped hold of the stick. Butch lifted the stick with the turtle still firmly attached to the end. Butch took the knife from his belt and cut off the head. Butch threw the stick with head attached into the mill pond. Butch picked up the turtle minus the head and took it to Mr. Houser.

Mr. Houser looked it over, "It's a good size but not a large turtle." Mr. Houser paid two dollars for the turtle.

Mr. Houser asked Butch if he would like to sample the soup

when he got it made. Mr. Houser always asked Butch the same question. He always got the same answer. With the shake of his head, with his blue eyes and freckled face, Butch would look at Mr. Houser and say, "Are you kidding me? I'd rather have the money."

Butch always turned away with a smile and two to three dollars in his pocket for a few minutes work and no out of pocket money invested.

*** LIFE IS FOR THE BIRDS ***

For a short time Butch was in the killing business, killing of pests. Every year the local FFA, Future Farmers of America, conducted a pest hunt, to get rid of the over population of sparrows, starlings, etc. The FFA boys got points towards awards for each pest they killed. Some of the FFA boys cheated a little and would pay Butch if he helped them out. They would pay him two cents for sparrows, five cents for starlings. Butch would take his BB gun and go down in front of the

86

business building and shoot sparrows off the top of the buildings.

The job was cut short when the business men in downtown complained to the local cop. Byron only had one cop. The business men didn't like Butch shooting the birds off the top of buildings. The building owners were afraid Butch was going to shoot out a window. He never did. It just didn't look good to have dead birds' bodies laying around the edge of the side walk.

The FFA boys only paid for the head, so Butch just gave them the head. Butch would hold the dead bird with his middle finger under the lower beak, and index finger behind the head and flip. Off goes the body and into the bag goes the head. You get what you pay for.

Butch now, less than fifteen years old, has completed his B.A. in business from the school of hard knocks, where the colors are black and blue and the motto is "not that we can do but that we have done". He has learned to find a product that someone needs or wants and is willing to pay a price for.

In the case of Skeeter and the rat business there was investment money in equipment, the traps, and he had to find a customer, who was Ted, the live bait guy to buy the rats. Skeeter helped train him in the skill of trapping rats. Butch never lost a dime on the rat business even though he gave the traps to Skeeter. Butch still turned a small profit.

In the chicken business with Del and Barry, Butch learned purchasing, pricing and competition. If he sold the chickens for less than the stores, people would buy chickens from him and the boys. Butch learned where he had to buy the chickens, the feed, and the material to finish the product. He and the boys negotiated free rental space, the coop, from Grandma.

Butch also learned the process for raising and preparing the chickens for market. And, of course, he learned about sales and distribution. Butch also learned to pick partners that he could trust, and would be able to contribute to the business. Butch and the boys made out quite well in the profit area.

In the bird business he found a need for little or no investment. BBs were cheap and he already had the BB gun. The bird shooting turned a very good profit for a while until the government stepped in, the village fathers and police!

The turtle business was best of all. No upfront investment. One hundred percent profit. Donald Trump take note.

Butch was off to the bank where he put most of his earnings. With the rest of his money he was off to the drugstore that didn't sell drugs, and had a cherry fountain coke with the boys. Cost: ten cents.

Butch didn't operate like General Motors. Thank God for that. He never went bankrupt! There were no government bailouts, no government take overs, no one ever lost a cent with ole Butch. Everyone made a little.

Butch didn't go to Harvard or Yale, just the school of hard knocks, where hard work, honesty, weren't just words. Don't steal, don't lie, don't cheat, treat people fair, was a way of life.

None of the partners shot themselves. However, later in life Del died of alcoholism. Del was in his mid-sixties. Things just didn't work out well for Del. He was just a step off from the straight and narrow. Del was above average in intelligence. He wasn't much of a book person. He quit school at sixteen or seventeen, worked, got married, and had a son who also became a drunk.

CHAPTER TWENTY

*** SUMMER GAMES ***

It was midsummer. It was hot, it was boring. It was about nine P.M. Butch, Dell, and Will were sitting on the bottom step of the stairs leading to Butch's parents' apartment.

"That was fun," Butch was referring to the water balloon fight the three of them had earlier in the evening. When it's summer, it's hot and you're bored stiff with no money, you have water balloon fights. It was the fifties. No swimming pools in the backyard, no air conditioning, just water and balloons.

Butch smiled, looked at the other two. Almost at the same time Will and Barry said, "Oh no you don't, we're not going to do it."

Will reminded Butch, "We talked about it before and we'll get in trouble. Worse than that we could get killed."

Barry added, "Worse than that I could lose my ass if my dad finds out."

Butch countered, "You're chicken, you're afraid."

Now just a minute! You might call a guy chicken, you might

say they're afraid, but no one, no one is both chicken and afraid to do something someone else is willing to do, not when your fourteen or fifteen years old, not in the mid-fifties, not in Byron.

The boys relented, "Okay, Butch what's your plan?"

"We'll simply walk up the steps to the back landing. Stand on the hand railing, climb up either the water drain or electric pipe, and shimmy up to the roof. It's only another six feet or so."

Del exclaimed, "You're crazy!"

"Are you going to do it or are you babies going home?"

That's all it took.

Let me set the stage for you. The boys are going to climb on top of the two story business buildings on main street in the dark, a very dangerous task.

Del and Barry both said, "Ok. How we gonna get the balloons to the top?"

Butch explained, "Simple. We'll fill them up on the ground. Carry them to the back porch. I'll climb on the roof first, then you two just toss them up to me. Then you two climb up."

Most of the store owners lived in the apartments over their

stores, or they rented the apartments. In any event, when you got to the landing there was a door that led into the apartments. The shades on the back windows and door were pulled most of the time. No one could see in, which meant no one could see out of the apartments.

The tricky part was standing on the handrail, about two and a half to three feet high, then grabbing onto the water drain and shinnying up the six feet or so. Very dangerous. Slip and it's a fifteen feet drop onto garbage cans or ground.

After you're on the roof, walk to the front of the buildings against the facade and wait for a car. When the car stops at the stop sign, loft two or three water balloons, and hit the car. The driver gets out and you loft two or three more balloons and the driver gets a bath. It's even better if the car is a convertible with the top down. It only happened once with a convertible. Take a quick peek, duck down below a three foot brick facade on top of the roof and get out of there. Remember be quiet as there are people watching *This is Your Life* on TV downstairs. Down the water drain, onto the handrail to the landing, down the stairs and run like hell for home!

The boys did this three or four times that summer, and never got caught. Well, you gotta do something when it's summer, it's hot and you're bored.

*** IT'S SO QUIET THAT YOU
CAN HEAR THE GRASS GROW ***

It was still summer, it was even hotter, and the boys are more bored than ever.

Butch recalled, "We sure got em with those water balloons, didn't we?"

The boys agreed, "Sure did." They look at Butch. He is smiling that same way that he smiles when he is about to be up to something.

Del moaned, "Ok Butch, what is it this time?

"Well if you don't want to do it, just say so."

Will, "Well what is it?"

Butch, "It's just too damned quiet, know what I mean?"

"It's ten o'clock at night. People are in bed, they have to go to work in the morning. We're supposed to be in bed."

"I still say it's too damned quiet tonight and every night," Butch complained.

Del inquired, "So what do you want to do, go around town and ring door bells and wake everybody up?"

Butch replied, "Something like that."

"Butch you really are getting crazier every day. We can't go around and ring all the door bells in town. It would take too long and we would get caught. Throwing a few balloons, stealing a few watermelons, even changing half the street signs in town is one thing but...."

Will laughed, "Yeah, that sign changing was real funny, it took them almost a week to put them back on the right streets."

Butch clarified, "It took them almost a week to find out the signs were changed. This is big, I mean real big. We pull this off, we're done for the summer."

Del sounded eager, "Do you mean it? No more horsing around? Just ease into fall?"

Butch agreed, "Yes, you going to do it?"

The boys, "Ok, what is it?"

"Will, you go to the Baptist Church. Dell, you go to the Methodist Church. I'll go to the fire station." Remember, Byron is a village of about six hundred sleepy eyed, hardworking people that go to bed early. The lay out is this: Both churches are just one block off main street and are only one block apart. The fire station is at the end of the row of stores, right on main street, one block south of the street the churches are on.

Back in the 50s the churches were left open as was the fire station. After all, who is going to rob a church? Of what? Bibles? Song books? Do you really think someone is going to steal the fire truck? Not back then. One thing to keep in mind, the fire department back then and even to this day is a volunteer fire department. When the fire siren sounds a dozen or more men jump out of bed and rush to the fire station. Starting to get the picture, aren't ya?

Butch continued, "When you get to your churches, count to ten and start ringing the bell. When I hear the bells ring, I'll push the fire alarm."

"No, no, you're crazy, that's going too far," the boys resisted.

Butch said, "We'll go down in history."

Will corrected, "We'll go to jail."

Dell added, "That would be the good part. Can you imagine

how pissed off the people will be, not to mention the firemen?"

Butch assured them, "We're not going to get caught. Will, you will be less than two blocks from home. Dell, one block, me across the street. The first firemens' feet won't hit the floor and we'll be home in bed." All three boys started to laugh.

Will stated, "God will get us for this."

Butch said, "Don't worry about God, worry about Jake." Jake was the town cop, the village street repairman, water hookup, etc. guy. Jake was Byron's answer to Barney Fife of Mayberry RFD.

Off they went. In less than a minute the bell at the Baptist Church started ringing, and a second or two later the Methodist bell sounded out, and a second later the fire siren went off.

The bells were the old large church bells and they were loud. The fire siren could be heard for a least a mile during the day when things were less quiet. On this night Butch said they could have heard the siren ring in the town of Durand seven miles away!

If you want the fire department, Lewie Small at the mortuary answered the phone. Lewie would push a button and a large fire siren on top of the fire station would scream out. The ten or so volunteer firemen would all go running to the fire hall. The men would run inside, grab a red clothespin off the desk, open the fire hall door, jump on the very old fire truck, and speed off sometimes breaking forty-five miles per hour.

After risking their lives, and they sometimes do, and ruining their clothes, the firemen would return to the fire station. Those firemen that have a red clothespin will be paid three dollars for their time and effort. Those that do not have a red clothespin get nothing. There are seven red clothespins. It is a way to run a low budget fire department.

Butch wondered if any of the volunteers just painted a clothespin red and kept it at home. No. Not in those days.

Lights were lit in every house in a matter of seconds. Women with curlers in their hair, bathrobes on, standing on their porches, wondering if the world was coming to an end. Firemen were out of their homes and in their cars racing to the fire station. The boys were home all covered up with visions of jail dancing in their heads. No one knew for sure who did it. There were only a handful of boys that would try such a thing.

Butch, Del, and Wills' parents never asked them if they were guilty. They didn't want to know.

CHAPTER TWENTY-ONE

*** VISIONS OF BEVERLY ***

The summer passed and time went by. Butch, now a young boy of sixteen, started to have feelings that he had back in the Utley community of, yeah, you remember, Beverly. The old hormones are working overtime. Every girl he saw he fantasized about.

Butch was not really a ladies' man. He got along with girls just fine and had several girls that were his friends, not girlfriends, just very good friends. Butch was really quite shy around girls.

As luck would have it, Butch met the second older woman in his life, Peggy. Butch was almost sixteen and Peggy was nineteen. Peggy graduated from Byron High School, had a car and a full time job.

Butch was introduced to Peggy by a mutual friend, Martha.

Martha was a young woman, twenty-four, married and had three boys who Butch sometimes babysits. Butch saw Martha almost everyday and they talked about life in general. Martha's husband, Georgio, owned a bar in the nearby town and worked second shift. He was your Italian stallion, tall, dark and very handsome. Georgio was something less than loyal to Martha and ran around with other women, played cards, and drank all night.

There was some talk that Butch and Martha had a romance going. There never was a physical relationship between them. They were just very good friends for many years.

Peggy was a blue eyed, blonde hair, pretty face girl with a very pleasant personality, slightly plump, with big boobs. That last part is pretty important to a sixteen year old boy. After a couple of meetings at Martha's apartment, Peggy invited Butch out to her house for a dance party that she threw every Saturday night.

Peggy's clean garage became a ballroom. Maybe not a ballroom, but it worked just fine. Peggy said she just has a couple of friends over, some of the guys and gals from around the lake that

Peggy lived on. They play some forty-fives and dance.

Peggy's house was located off a dirt road, down a narrow lane that resembles a cow path. The house sat on the edge of Myers Lake, a very isolated location where things can happen and no one would know.

Peggy lived with her mother, Ellen, a brother named Benny age twelve, two half-brothers, Neddie, nine, and Dominic, seven, and a stepfather named Ned. Did you catch it? Ned and Neddie, stepbrother and stepfather? Again, it doesn't take much to figure out a family tree in Byron. Butch says people in Byron go to a family reunion to find a date.

The first Saturday night at Peggy's dance party, Butch saw an old friend that he went to school with at Utley. Gordie was two years older than Butch and they were in the same grade a couple of years. Gordie had a little trouble with school and failed a couple grades.

Butch and Gordie's first reunion at Myers Lake was a couple of years earlier. Gordie's older brother had a cottage across from Myers Lake and Gordie would spend most of the summers there. Butch was thirteen and Gordie fifteen when they first met at Myers Lake.

Butch asked Gordie if he still played any baseball. At fifteen,

Gordie was five feet ten inches, one hundred sixty-five pounds and very athletic built, light brown hair, almost blonde, blue eyed, nice looking boy. Now two years later Gordie was about six feet two inches and one hundred eighty pounds and even better looking.

After a few Saturday nights, Butch and Peggy started getting closer while dancing, a little kiss here, a little kiss there.

One night, Butch and Gordie went to the little beer and wine store for some pop and chips. As they arrived back at Peggy's house, Butch stopped the car and Gordie looked over at Butch with a serious look and said, "What about you and Peggy?"

Butch thought, "Oh crap. Peggy and Gordie are a thing and Gordie isn't liking what he has been seeing."

For three real good reasons this was not a good situation for Butch. One, Gordie was Butch's friend and friends don't move in on a friend's girl. Second, Gordie had a short fuse for a temper. Third, Butch was small and Gordie was big.

Butch with his lighting fast mind, "What do you mean, Gordie?

Gordie answered, "You know, you and Peggy?" Butch's eyes got big, a lump in his throat, he knew that Gordie could get real violent, out of control with his temper.

"Listen, Gordie, I didn't know you and Peggy were a couple."

Gordie threw back his head and laughed. "We're not, that's just it, go for it, she's a nice girl."

Quite relieved and confused Butch said, "That makes me feel a lot better, but if it's not Peggy who is it you're after at the dance?"

Guys generally didn't go to dances to dance, they went to meet girls. There's wasn't that many good looking girls at Peggy's dance parties.

Gordie answered, "Ellen." That would be Peggy's mother. Now it's time for Butch to throw back his head and laugh. Butch looked over at Gordie. Gordie wasn't laughing.

"That's right, I'm in love with Peggy's mother. Have been for a while now," Gordie said.

Life goes on in a normal fashion for Butch, whatever normal is.

There's Butch and Peggy, Gordie and Ellen, Saturday night dances, Peggy's brother and two half-brothers. And then there's Ned, the stepfather.

One fine Saturday afternoon Butch drove out to see Peggy.

Butch knocked on the door and Ned, Ellen's husband, hollered out,

"Come in." Ned is an average size guy, a little on the heavy side, ten

plus years older than Ellen. Ned was just starting to lose a little hair on

top, wore glass, dressed well. One thing you notice right off when you

met Ned was he didn't have a tooth in his head, not one, none the less,

he was very outgoing and spoke well. Ned was quite an intelligent

man. His occupation was what we would call today a telemarketer. He

traveled with a company that went from city to city selling advertising

and tickets for police fund raisers. Ned was very good at what he did

and maked a good living at it.

Butch found Ned sitting at the kitchen table. He and Ned got

along quite well. They joked and kidded a lot in spite of their age

difference. Butch sat down across from Ned and said something real

intelligent like "How they hanging, Ned?" You just can't beat Butch's

command of the English language.

Ned was sitting with his hands palms down on the table with a

serious, sad sort of look on his face. He asked, "What do you know

about that?" He nodded his head toward the window that overlooked

Myers Lake.

Butch looked out the window and there, on the water's edge, stood Gordie and Peggy's mother, Ellen. Butch's head snapped back and he looked at Ned. Butch's eyes were as big as saucers, his heart was beating fast. Just then Ned lifted both of his hands from the table. And there pointing straight at Butch was a pistol. The hole in the end of the pistol looked as big as a cannon.

Now Butch's heart was about to jump out of his body. Ned was looking straight at Butch.

Butch in his ever quick mind replied, "What do you mean?"

Ned nodded his head towards the window again, and said, "Those two."

Butch, "I don't know anything."

Ned stood up, picked up the pistol from the table, put the pistol in his pocket, turned from the table, walked out the front door. Butch never saw Ned again.

As for Butch and Peggy, they broke up within a year. Peggy found someone that was more her age and in more of a marrying mode.

A year or two after Butch and Peggy broke up, Gordie and Ellen moved. There was apparently an argument between the two of

104

them. Ellen made some remark about Gordie. Gordie, in a fit of

rage, left the living room where Ellen and Peggy's three brothers were

sitting. Gordie returned with a twelve-gauge shot gun and said, "So you

think that's funny, watch this." He put the shotgun barrel in his mouth

and pulled the trigger, blowing the top of his head off. Gordie was

twenty years old at the time.

Sometime later, Ellen bumped into a guy named Dane. As odd

as it may seem, Dane was also from the Utley Community. Dane went

to school with Butch's brother Jack and lived just one street behind

Butch and Jack.

Dane had worked for Butch's father Harold, when Harold had

first started the machine shop on Brown Street and later moved the shop

to Byron. Dane moved from the Utley area out to a small town close to

Byron.

Dane and Ellen met at a watering hole, not far from Byron, got

to know each other and some sort of a romance ensued. One night after

leaving the bar, Dane and Ellen got into his car and started driving.

They both had been drinking too much and Dane was driving too fast,

missed a curve and hit a tree, killing Ellen on the spot. Dane survived with minor injuries.

One of Peggy's half-brothers, Dominic, the youngest, was ten or eleven when he saw Gordie shoot himself. Some years later. as a young adult, Dominic shot himself. Butch never knew what the circumstances were.

Butch survived the breakup with Peggy with a broken heart. It mended quickly with the help of several life experiences.

CHAPTER TWENTY-TWO

*** HONESTY IS THE BEST POLICY ***

One such experience could be titled *honesty is the best policy,*

or is it? Not always, according to Butch. Remember be honest, tell the

truth, even if it cost you.

It was in the spring of Butch's eleventh grade. Baseball season.

Butch had made the varsity as a sophomore and was likely to be the

starting second baseman his junior year. There wasn't much

competition, just one boy a year younger than Butch, Robby.

Robby was about the same size as Butch. Robby was a good

ball player, but just a little behind Butch. Butch was the small guy you

need on the team. The one that's fast, quick, very athletic. Every team

can use one. You don't need two.

Butch had already established himself at Byron. He was the

second baseman and the point guard on the basketball team. Butch was

often the high point scorer on the basketball team. In one junior varsity

game, he scored twenty-one of Byron's twenty-eight points. Things

were looking good.

107

Butch later had a falling out with the varsity basketball coach that year and quit basketball. That should have had nothing to do with baseball as the baseball coach was a different person.

Then there was Robby. Robby was a nice guy and liked playing basketball and baseball, too. Just one thing, Butch was a year older and already in place. It didn't look like Robby was going to play any basketball or baseball until his senior year. That didn't sit well with Robby's father.

Robby's father was one of the businessmen in Byron. He owned a local retail store. He also happened to be a former graduate of Byron High School and had played a lot of sports in his time. He also wanted Robby to do the same.

Robby's dad, Mr. Houser, was very close with the head coach at Byron. He and Mr. Munson, the basketball coach, went to the same church. On Sunday after church, Coach Munson and Robby's family had dinner together at Robby's house.

It was pretty well known that Butch smoked and was a bit on the rough side. Butch wore a black leather jacket with zippers on the arms and pockets and combed his hair DA style. All the cool guys, or

108

the ones that thought they were cool, combed their hair DA style. Butch wore black leather boots with heel plates that made a clicking sound when he walked down the hallways of good ole Byron High.

Although Butch dressed like a hood and ran with boys two to three years older than himself, he was quite well liked and accepted by his classmates and teachers. Butch was just Butch. He would sign his school papers "Butch", not his given name. Sometimes he would draw a little duck smoking a pipe. The teacher would say, "That's just Butch." Everything was okay, except for Mr. Houser and Coach Munson.

Just as the baseball season started Coach Munson called Butch into his room. Butch thought this can't be good! Coach Munson, the head coach, and Coach Sides, the varsity baseball coach were there. Coach Sides and Butch got along fine. Coach Munson asked Butch to have a seat.

Coach Munson accused, "We know you're smoking and smoking is a violation of team rules." Butch didn't say a word. "I SAID we know you are smoking and smoking is a team violation."

Butch replied, "How do you know that? Have you seen me

smoking?"

"No, someone told me."

"Who?" Butch knew that very few people actually saw him smoking and they were friends he could trust.

"It doesn't matter who. I can tell you it was an adult though."

Let's see, what adult would have any reason to squeal to the coach that Butch was smoking? Maybe Mr. Houser, Robby's dad, who by the way, was the same person Butch used to sell turtles to for turtle soup.

"It doesn't matter. Do you or don't you smoke?"

Butch's dad always said, don't lie, steal, cheat or he would knock the crap out of him. Let's see crap kick or tell the truth?

Butch answered, "Yes."

"That's it, you're done!"

"Coach, I promise I'll quit if you just give me a chance." This would have been a good lesson for Butch and for all the other boys. Let Butch play ball, but make him pay some kind of penitence. Run laps, miss the first game, apologize to the team for misconduct. Oh no, not Coach Munson, he didn't like Butch all that well and he did like Robby and Robby's dad.

Coach Munson, "No, you're out of playing any sports at Byron for one year.

"One year!" Today a kid gets a girl pregnant, robs the corner party store, can't spell his own name, and all he has to do is say "I'm sorry," or get a lawyer and sue.

Butch turned to Coach Sides and asked, "What about baseball?" Butch thought that Coach Munson meant that he couldn't run track or play basketball for a year.

Coach Sides started to say something and Coach Munson interrupted. "I'm the head coach here and I say he's through for a year." That pretty much ended Butch's ball playing career at Byron.

Later, Butch was told by the other boys that Munson and Sides had quite a discussion over the matter. Munson won.

There was a lot of smoking, drinking, etc. by other ball players at good ole Byron. None confessed to anything.

Good lesson taught by Coach Munson. In years to come Munson had several jobs and had trouble on all of them. Coach Sides went on to do coaching and fared quite well.

CHAPTER TWENTY-THREE

*** GETTING OVER PEGGY ***

Getting over Peggy, losing out on playing sports. What's left?

Girls. As we said, Butch wasn't much of a ladies' man, but he did have

a lot of friends that were girls.

Two of Butch's girl buddies, as they were known, were Beth

and Lana. Beth was the one Butch could tell dirty jokes with like she

was one of the boys. Beth was better than average looking, slender

with a very nice smile, and was a little taller than Butch. Most

everybody was.

A few years after Butch and Beth graduated, Beth would bring

her two daughters over and visit with Butch and Diana. Beth's two girls

would play with Butch's daughter, Sherri. Beth and Butch would visit

and talk about old times. Diana would go about her house work and

sort of look after the girls playing. Diana was never intimidated with

Butch having his girl buddies. She knew, and it was true, they were just

that, buddies.

After several months the visits from Beth stopped. She was

having a little marital trouble and life just changes as life does.

Some years passed and Butch found out that one of Beth's daughters, just seventeen years old, had been murdered. She was found along with her boyfriend, their hands tied behind their backs and duct tape over their mouths. Both had been shot in the back of the head. It was thought to be a drug deal gone bad.

Butch and Beth started talking with each other several years later. Well, not talking, but e-mailing. Beth had remarried and was doing well.

*** LIFE GOES ON ***

Lana was the one Butch really would have liked to have had more as a lover than a friend. Lana was a nice looking girl, not beautiful, but good looking. Lana was very popular with the boys and had a good reputation. Very bright girl!

Butch would talk with Lana for an hour or more at a time. Of course, it wasn't hard for Butch to talk an hour with anyone. Lana and Butch would talk about everything.

Lana was always there to help Butch with his school work. When Butch had to give a book report he would ask her if she had read any good books lately. She knew what he was up to. She would tell Butch about a book she read. He would listen. Lana would give him a good overview of the book, name of the author, main characters, events, etc. Butch would stand up in front of the class and give a report as if he read the book cover to cover. Mrs. Throop, the English teacher, would ask him a few questions about the book but Butch pretty much had it covered. Lana did a great job.

Back in the days Butch went to Byron High School, each student had to buy their own books. Most students bought used books to keep the cost down. Butch had a better idea on how to keep the cost of buying books down. Don't buy any. When it came to buying books for school or a Coke to drink, guess which one won.

When it came time to make out his senior year schedule of classes Butch decided to take fourth year English. Fourth year English was broken down into two parts, English literature and speech. Butch was a good talker. Speech class was right up his alley. English literature not so much.

Butch never did anything on time. His middle name should have been Procrastinator. That's what he did best. His motto was "never do today what you can put off till tomorrow." He could have been president of the National Procrastinators Club of America but he just couldn't get around to it. During one of Mrs.Throop's classes, Butch was asked to read something from his literature book. He turned to the person next to him and asked to borrow their book.

Mrs. Throop, "Butch, don't you have a literature book of your own?"

"No, I forgot to buy one. I will buy one tomorrow."

"Why bother?"

So he didn't. Butch passed the class with his usual C.

CHAPTER TWENTY-FOUR

*** THE REAL THING ***

Through all the nonsense and buddy type girlfriends, there was one girl. There's always one. Remember when you were in school that certain boy or girl that you used to day dream about. The one that was just out of reach. For the girls it was the captain of the football team, the all American dashing hero. For the guys, it was that knockout blonde with the big boobs. The cheerleader. The one that went with the captain of the football team.

Butch had one of his own, Diana. She was a true knockout, long black hair, hazel eyes, nice smooth olive complexion. Beautiful smile, and I mean a real set of, well nice build, five-foot three, one hundred twenty pounds, thirtysix-twentyfour-thirtyeight. Get the picture?

Butch first noticed Diana when she was in the ninth grade and he was in the tenth grade. Diana had just moved from Flint. She stood out from all the other girls and just got better over time. Of course, Diana didn't take any notice of Butch. Diana was a cheerleader, was on the Queen's court at homecoming, and in the senior high school play. All the boys wanted to date Diana.

Butch started dating Diana's best friend, Juanita. Juanita was also a very nice looking girl, one year younger than Diana. Juanita's older brother, Terry, was in the same class as Butch.

The romance between Butch and Juanita was just a hug and an innocent kiss. Butch's goal was Diana and he knew he couldn't reach his goal without some help, and Juanita was that help. Juanita really didn't mind helping Butch with his plan. She liked Butch but only as a friend.

Juanita was Butch's John Alden. John Alden was a character in Longfellow's poem "Courtship of Miles Standish". John Alden was supposed to ask for the hand of a maiden for a friend who was too shy to do it himself. Long story short, John wound up with the maiden.

Oh! By the way, there really was a John Alden in Butch's class at Byron, not as fortunate as Longfellow's John Alden, never the less John Alden in name. One day a couple of guys in Butch's class, we won't say who, were playing around. They hung John Alden out the second story window of the study hall, holding him by his ankles. Everyone, including Johnny, was having a good laugh, when all a sudden the study hall teacher walked into the room and noticed what was going on. She said, "LET GO OF HIM!" The boys hanging onto Johnny looked at each other and said "Okay," and let go. Johnny fell into a bush and came out with a lot of scratches. The boys got detention for a week.

With Juanita's help and Butch showing up at the right times with the right smile and the right line, he was ready.

Butch just didn't have the courage. I mean, after all, Diana and Butch, no one gave it a chance, not even Butch. Butch would get in his 1954 Willis and drive up and down the road Diana lived on. Diana lived out in the country on a dirt road.

One day Butch got up the nerve to pull into Diana's driveway but at the last minute he chickened out. He put the old Willis in reverse

118

and started to leave. Wouldn't you know it, the milkman pulled in behind Butch. Diana must have seen Butch stranded in front of the milk truck. She came out the door and in a half run was at the door of the Willis before he could move.

Butch doesn't really remember what was said by either Diana or him. All he remembers is that he did ask her out on a date and Diana said yes.

Butch said it would be a double date with his friend Frank and his steady girl and they would be going bowling. Frank, was three years older than Butch and had already graduated from high school and was working at General Motors. All this aside, Frank was mild compared to the bunch Butch used to run with. Double dates were easy first dates especially whenever one knew everyone else, the pressure of entertaining would not be entirely on Butch's shoulders. Bowling was a good date. He wouldn't have to worry about too much necking or too little or how good he was. All the necking would be a simple goodnight kiss. Diana also realized the setup and was probably glad for it.

Butch may not have been the smartest kid on the block but he knew his way around the corner. This was going to be a make or break date. Move too fast, it's over, not be cool, it's over, and the goodnight kiss better be the best or it's over.

Butch didn't think there was a snowballs chance in hell he was going to pull this off. All he could think of for the next three days before the date is what he was going to do. The word got out faster than if you would have put it on radio or TV. Butch was taking Diana out on Saturday. The conversation must have gone like this:

"You got to be kidding, Butch and Diana?"

"Diana must have had an open night and didn't want to stay home."

"What did Butch do, hold a gun to her head?"

That's what Butch was thinking. His friends all said, "We couldn't believe it. Go for it. You got the shot you've been waiting for, don't mess it up."

The night of the date, Diana must have been thinking, "What was I thinking of when I said yes?"

Butch was getting ready for the challenge. He couldn't eat his supper and almost threw up several times. He picked out his clothes with care. He was over the black leather jacket, engineer boots bit, but he still had a big wave in his hair and wore a modified DA.

Butch wasn't running with the older guys anymore, he ran with people more his own age. He had experience over people his own age. He had already been where they were going.

Butch's wardrobe was dress pants, dress shoes. He had a dozen plus sweaters, V neck, round neck, and the shawl. You name he had it. The shawl sweater was in. The shawl referred to the neck of the sweater. The collar sort of rolled around the back of your neck and it was thick and soft. It was in, and it was cool. Best of all, Butch looked good in them.

Butch was now part of the clique. All schools have cliques, even Byron. Some cliques are good, some are not. He was in the good clique, he was in the sports clique, the so called cool guys. Butch didn't have much going for him but he had a certain amount of class. He dressed well and ran with the right crowd, knew a million jokes, some clean. And he had hair. That's right, hair. In the late 1950s rock and roll, Elvis the Pelvis, Brill Cream for hair.

Butch must have gone through a tube of Brylcreem every two weeks. Brylcreem was a white, mild greasy hair cream you put on your hand and run it through your hair. After you comb your hair there wasn't a breeze, a wind, there wasn't a hurricane that was going to blow your hair out of place.

Frank picked Butch up and they were off on the date.

Frank's girlfriend, Norma, who knew Butch quite well and liked him, said "Butch you're really a big boy now."

Butch shot back, "You're real funny, real funny!"

When they got to Diana's house, Butch got out of the car and started walking towards the house, when all of a sudden out of the door pops Diana's half-brother Dan. Dan was a skinny little kid, about seven or eight. Out of his mouth comes, "My daddy doesn't like you."

Before Butch could think he snapped back, "Well tell your dad I don't like him either." Nice way to get on the good side of the family.

The rest of the night went great. Butch showed his athleticism and was the best of the four bowling. He put on his best performance, did everything right. He could have won the academy award for best actor. The Oscar was his.

The ride home was small talk and laughs. Next, the walk to the door and the kiss goodnight. This is it, the make or break it time, everything else led to this. Move too fast, it's over. One nice kiss,

no tongue, nice kiss maybe a light second kiss. Don't slobber all over.

Don't stumble on the way to the door. Don't talk too much. Most of

all, try not to crap your pants. Talk about being nervous. Anything

could happen at the door.

Diana said, "I had a good time." What else was she going to

say? "I can't wait to get into the house"?

"Me too." Then he kissed Diana goodnight. One of his best, be

had been practicing for a week on the back of his hand.

Now let's stop right here. Ole Butch had been around a little.

He had Beverly and the girls back at Utley. Although they really didn't

know too much about sex they did come close and they necked a lot.

There was Peggy, the older woman in his life.

Then there was Sally. Oh yes, there was Sally! Sally was a

very nice looking Baptist girl. Can't beat a hot sweaty Baptist girl!

Sally was a great necker, that's as far as it went. But neck, she

could! Butch and Sally double-dated with Frank and his steady, the

same Frank and the same steady Butch and Diana dated with except that

time the date was at a drive-in movie.

Butch had no idea what the movies were about. Back then they had double features back to back, cartoons, coming attractions, these things could go on for four plus hours. The necking with Sally got so hot and heavy she had to take off her glasses so they wouldn't get broke. She couldn't see out of them anyway, they were too steamed over. Frank's date even mentioned, "Maybe Butch should come up for air every once and a while." All Butch remembered was the movie started and ended.

Sally said she was only trying to show Butch a good time! Believe me, Butch had a good time! He said he had a pucker on his lips for a week. He couldn't talk, all he could do was whistle. Frank's date said she had never seen anything like that on a first date in her life. All Butch would say after that night was "praise the Lord and hallelujah for pretty little Baptist girls."

By the way Diana was Baptist too. How lucky can one guy get? All this to say the kiss with Diana went well. In parting, Butch said to Diana, "Maybe we can do this again."

And Diana said, "Yes."

CHAPTER TWENTY-FIVE

*** SCHOOL DAYS, SCHOOL DAYS.

OH NO, THEY'RE GONE! ***

June, 1960, Butch graduated from Byron Agriculture High School. Butch was twenty third in his class of forty one with a C average and proud of it. Most people didn't think he would graduate, let alone get a C average, not his father, brother, most of all his mother. Butch didn't give anyone a reason to. He didn't study. He did just enough to get by. Butch's mother didn't give much encouragement, just the opposite. When he went out for basketball she laughed and said he was too short. We know how that went.

When Butch was going to take typing in high school Edna said, "Oh no, that is way too difficult." You had to memorize all the letters without looking. Butch took two years of typing in school, typed fifty

five words a minute with three errors or less in a five minute test
and that very good on a manual typewriter. He received an A in both
years of high school typing. He enrolled at Flint Jr. College and took
two semesters of typing there and received an A both semesters.

Butch believed his mother's lack of confidence in him came
from her own inability to do well in school. Whatever was difficult for
her, she felt was difficult for most people. Don't misunderstand, there
was no doubt in Butch's mind that his mother loved him. She had lived
through the Great Depression of the thirties, and it took its toll on her
spirit and on her physically.

Next was college. College! What do you mean college? Butch
barely got through high school.

About midway through Butch's second semester of his senior
year, Ned Huntz, Butch's high school principal, called him into his
office. Butch thought he was in trouble, after all, why else would the
principal call him in? He couldn't think of a thing he had done wrong
lately. Butch walked into the principal's office.

Mr. Huntz ordered, "Sit down, Butch, I would like to talk to
you about school next year."

Butch thought, "School next year? You mean I'm not graduating?" If a student was getting grades that might not let them graduate, Mr. Huntz would call them into his office and give them a pep talk. "If you don't do better you will not graduate." Or something like that. Usually it was earlier in the year. About three or four classmates of Butch's had already been called on the carpet.

Butch didn't say anything, just sat there looking up at Mr. Huntz. Mr. Huntz was a young guy in his middle thirties, tall, wore black horn rimmed glasses.

Mr. Huntz thought Butch should attend college. Butch thought, "Are you kidding me, give me a break! I'm the guy who didn't buy a twelfth grade literature book! The guy who had Lana tell him about a book she read so he could give a book report. The guy who had Danny Belcure do all his art drawings so he could pass art class. And you think I should go to college? You got to be kidding!"

Butch asked, "You know I'm not a good student, that I just slipped by?"

"I know more than you think, Butch. I know that if you tried, you could do well in college. I know, for instance, you help Timmy

Mott." Timmy Mott was an oversized eighth grader that was having trouble with his math. Butch was asked to help Timmy.

Butch had joined the Future Teachers of America, an organization that introduced high school students to teaching. Butch thought if he was to go to college he would like to coach baseball and teach history in high school. Butch never gave college a thought. The only subject he really liked and did well at besides phys ed was history.

Mrs. Hubert, the Future Teachers sponsor, asked Butch if he would help Timmy with his math. Butch also wasn't too bad at math. He didn't know it, but some of the teachers believed he had potential.

Butch found out that Timmy could work out math problems if they were not story problems. Give Timmy a row to add, multiply, or divide, and he could do it. Put the math problem into story form, Timmy was lost. Timmy's problem was not math, but reading. He could not say the ABCs correctly. Up to the eighth grade Timmy was able to get around reading. Mrs. Hubert and the other teachers knew Timmy didn't read well, but they didn't know it was to that extent.

Mr. Huntz knew about Butch helping Timmy during conversations with his teachers. Mr. Huntz said, "Butch if you apply

yourself and want to bad enough, you can do college work."
Butch never had anyone believe in him before, not the way Mr. Huntz
did.

Butch's grades weren't good enough to get into a major college
or university so he enrolled at Flint Jr. College. The tuition was low and
Flint J.C. was only twenty five miles from home. A full year's tuition
with books was less than eight hundred dollars. Butch's dad said he
would pay him twenty-five dollars a week, pay for his tuition, and five
dollars a week to ride back and forth to school with Greg and Barb.
Greg and Barb were two kids Butch graduated with.

That seemed fair. Work forty hours a week in the machine
shop, get twenty-five dollars a week. Let's see, that works out to just
under sixty-two cents per hour, but let's not forget the eight hundred
dollars in books, tuition, and five dollars a week for transportation.
Let's see, five dollars a week for thirty-two weeks in a school year
comes out to one hundred and sixty dollars plus the eight hundred in
tuition and books that comes to nine hundred and sixty dollars, divide
that by the twelve weeks Butch worked, that comes to eighty dollars a
week, plus the twenty-five in cash. Bingo, one hundred and five dollars

per week! Not bad pay in the summer of 1960.

College didn't go well for Butch. Although Flint Jr. College was a small community college, Butch felt overwhelmed. He only knew Rob and Barb, and he was not in the clique, he wasn't sure of himself.

Butch still hadn't learned how to study, schedule study time, and play time. He got the play time down but not the study time. Through the first semester his grades were fair at best, D+ C-. The second semester was worse. Butch took an accounting class. He had a year of bookkeeping in high school and received a B. Somehow he got off the track about midsemester. He should have gone to his teacher and asked for help. But he didn't, and after some time Butch dropped the class and received an I for incomplete. Butch could still have salvaged the grade by going to the teacher, but again he let it go and the I turned to an E, a four credit hour E. That was the killer. Butch's C-average now turned into a weak D. It was kindergarten all over again. Butch quit college, something he regretted the rest of his life. Lesson learned, don't quit anything.

Butch did receive some good advice from Barb. Butch and

Barb became friends during the year they rode back and forth to Flint J.C. Barb's advice was simple, "Why don't you turn the I into a better grade by taking the class over?" This actually was great advice. That could have changed Butch's life for the better. He would have graduated from college or at least he would have stayed in school longer and who knows?

Who listens to advice anyway? Why would Butch listen to Barb? She was only a straight A student. She eventually graduated from not only Flint Jr. College, but also the University of Michigan, majoring in elementary education. Listening is good advice, act upon it.

Out of high school, not going back to college, what's next? WORK! No training, not much schooling. Ah, good ole dad who just happens to own a machine shop! Bingo! Job!

CHAPTER TWENTY-SIX

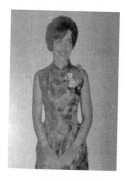

*** DIANA ***

Butch worked by day and chased Diana by night. It liked to killed him. Butch's dad always seemed to know when he was out the latest. The next morning Butch got the job that was hardest to do.

On September 2, 1961 Butch put a halt to the work all day, run all night. He married Diana.

Butch to this day cannot believe Diana said yes. Maybe she was answering another question.

Diana turned eighteen on May 26, 1961, graduated June, 1961, went to work for the State of Michigan June, 1961, got married in September 1961, and got pregnant in 1961. Could say Diana had a big year in 1961.

Diana was a very good looking, bright person. She was exceptionally talented in clerical skills. She could type over eighty words a minute on a manual typewriter. That would be even more on a computer keyboard. She could take a hundred twenty words a minute in shorthand. Diana was offered scholarships to Central Michigan University and to Flint Jr. College to pursue business.

Diana's high school principal, Mr. Huntz, the same high school principal that thought Butch could make it in college, advised Diana to take the State of Michigan job she was offered instead of going to college. Sounds like Mr. Huntz was wrong twice. However, taking the state job was the best for Diana, in the end.

Diana had a lot going for her. She had brains and looks. The downside was her family life. Diana lived with her mother Eleanor, Tate, her stepfather, two sisters, two half-sisters, and half-brother.

Diana's stepfather, Tate, was the stepfather from hell. He treated all the family members equal, rotten. Diana's biological father, Bob, was a military man who served twenty-seven years in the Army. He was ten years older than Diana's mother. Those ten years made a big difference to Eleanor as time went by. She apparently married him for two reasons. He looked nice in his uniform and she wanted to get out on her own. Tate became the other guy between Diana's mother and father. The triangle became very violent and resulted in divorce.

Tate seldom worked and the family lived off welfare. In the mid-1950s welfare was not quite as giving as now. You could get food commodities such as butter, sugar, flour, basics which you had to go to the welfare office and stand in line to receive. People living on welfare in the 50s were very much looked down on as second class citizens. If you had any pride you were ashamed.

One apartment Diana's family lived in had mold growing on the walls. Diana or her mother would have to go across the street to a gas station ladies room and fill pails of water to drink and do dishes.

Tate didn't trust anyone. He checked tire marks in the driveway to see if anyone had been to the house during his absence. Also upon his return, he would go to the radio, put his hand on it to see if it was warm. In this way he could tell if anyone had played the radio while he was out. He read all outgoing mail, mailing only the ones he wanted to, and confiscated incoming letters.

Diana's father paid child support for Diana and her two sisters. Diana's mother would tell Diana to write her dad and ask for more money. When he would send extra money, the stepfather would take the money and apply it to his own child support. Her stepfather would throw away Diana's letters, all except those asking for money.

After a while Diana's father stopped writing and sending extra money, thinking that all Diana wanted was the money. Her dad didn't know that Diana didn't spend or have any of the money spent on her or the other girls. She no longer saw her dad from about age ten.

After Diana and Butch were married she tried many times to find out where her father was. She asked aunts and uncles directly related to her dad but they were sworn to secrecy. One of Diana's cousins had seen her dad several times over the years. He would not tell Diana anything about her father.

In 2002 Diana got a letter from her stepmother, Cilly, telling Diana that her father had passed away.

Two years later Butch and Diana went to the state of Washington, where her stepmother lived. Diana had a nice visit and got some closure.

Cilly was born in Austria and met Diana's father when he was stationed in Germany with the Army. Cilly married Diana's father in 1956.

When the money stopped coming from her dad things got worse off financially. Diana's family moved from Flint to Byron, four miles out of town, two miles down a dirt road. The living room couch was the back seat of a 1946 Buick and the picture on the wall, a glued picture puzzle. The girls' dresser drawers were orange crates stood on end. These were constructed of balsa wood and wire with a shelf in the middle, and their mother made a curtain to hide the contents. Diana was about fourteen at this time and was already starting to develop into a young woman. She had one bra that she had to hand wash before using each time. She had to use safety pins to hold it together. Most other meager furnishings in the house were used and given to them. They did get a TV, but weren't allowed to watch it during the stepfather's absence, the same for the radio. They did not subscribe to a newspaper. The radio was played only when Tate was home, and had to be played so softly the girls had to put their ear up against the speaker.

No friends visited inside the house. Juanita, Diana's friend down the road, was the only one allowed inside house. Diana's sisters were still too young to have company from school spending the night.

Later, when Diana was allowed to date boys, the boys could come to the back porch. The back porch was a large enclosed wooden structure that was about to fall down. The boys were not allowed in the house.

Tate and Eleanor were heavy into drinking. They would put the kids in the car and drive to Pinconning. Pinconning is a small town in the thumb area of Michigan on Lake Huron. It is well known for its cheese. Under the pretense of going on a nice drive of forty miles or so and getting some Pinconning cheese, Diana knew this meant her stepfather and her mother were going to get drunk and that would lead to arguing and fighting. Tate would beat up Eleanor.

On one trip it really got out of hand. Tate beat Eleanor until she was unconscious. He beat her until her nose bled, her lips were cut, and both eyes were black and she was bleeding vaginally. She wound up in a deep ditch unconscious. While the beating was going on, Diana slipped out of the car with all five siblings. Diana ran up the road and

137

toward a bridge, hoping to hide. It was in the dead of night on a stretch of highway without any light. When Diana saw head lights of an oncoming car she stepped into the road waving her hand to have them stop and help her and her brother and sisters. The first car slowed down, looked, and continued on. After some time, a man and his wife stopped and drove Diana and her siblings to Pinconning to the Police Department in the next town. Tate was already there. Somehow Tate convinced the police everything was okay. Diana's mother remained in the car outside the police office beaten up. Diana and the other kids were too scared to say anything. Tate walked out of the police station with a big smile on his face and six crying children.

Tate was never physically abusive to the girls, just mentally abusive. He was physically abusive to Dan. Dan was Tate's biological son with Eleanor. You would think Tate would treat Dan the best, but no.

Dan was having trouble learning to use the toilet. Once in a while poor Dan would slip and go in his diaper. Tate would beat on Dan so hard he would leave hand prints on Dan's back for a week. Diana once tried to intervene and Tate told her she had better shut up or she'd get the same.

Diana would occasionally clean house for an old woman. Diana would get a dollar or two for her labor. You know who got the money, good ole Tate. After Tate took the money a few times, Diana caught on, and when the lady paid her two dollars, Diana would tell Tate she only got one.

Diana, being the oldest and looking a great deal like her dad, took most of the mental abuse from Tate. He would tell Diana that she wasn't very smart although she was always on the honor roll at school. When Diana tried out for the cheerleading team, Tate said she wouldn't make it. She did. Tate would not take Diana to games so she could cheer nor would he pick her up so she had to find a ride. Somehow the kids in school knew some of the problems Diana was having at home so they or their parents would give Diana a ride home.

Byron was a small farm town that lacked for culture and entertainment. One way to fill the void was the junior and senior class stage plays. The school plays were under the direction of Mrs. Throop, who put a lot of extra unpaid time into each one. The plays were a big deal, and to be chosen was an honor, like making the cheerleading team or even one of the ball teams. To a lot of kids this was their only time to shine. Mrs. Throop knew all the students very well. Anyone who took ninth through twelfth grade English or art class had Mrs. Throop for their teacher.

Diana was in four years of English and three years of art. She was one of Mrs. Throop's best art students. Diana's water colors were so good that Mrs. Throop asked if she could take one or two home for her personal pleasure. Mrs. Throop said to Diana, "Take the paintings home first and have your mother look at them. If she wants them, of course, let her have them. I'm sure she will want one or both."

Diana took the paintings home and told her mother that if she didn't want them Mrs. Throop did. Eleanor's reply was, "Where would they fit here?" Diana gave them to Mrs. Throop.

Mrs. Throop asked Diana if she wanted to be in the senior play. Diana said she would like to but didn't know if she would have a way back and forth for rehearsal and the play. Mrs. Throop said not to worry she would help her with a ride. Diana got the second lead and was quite good. Tate nor Eleanor attended. What a surprise!

In the spring of Diana's senior year, just before graduation,

Diana took a civil service test to work for the State of Michigan. Diana scored very high and got an interview. The interview was in a town about twenty miles from Byron. Of course Tate said he wouldn't take her for the interview. He said she wouldn't get the job anyway.

When Diana told her business teacher, Mrs. Freeman, she couldn't go to the interview because she didn't have a ride, Mrs. Freeman contacted the principal, Mr. Huntz. As luck would have it, there was a senior class field trip going right by her place of the interview. Mr. Huntz said Diana could ride with them and after the interview, wait and ride back. Couldn't do that today! Too much liability! Somebody would sue somebody! Diana was hired and everyone on the bus was happy for her and clapped their hands and cheered!

The school year of 1960-61, Diana made the cheerleading team, performed in the senior play, and interviewed and was hired for a Civil Service job before graduation. And all while good ole Tate said Diana couldn't do any of it. You think he would have learned something by now, but no he didn't.

Wait a minute, Diana got the job and the job was twenty miles away from home. She had no car and no driver's license. Diana was not allowed to take drivers education in school even though it was free, unlike today. Diana was also not allowed to do any of the cooking. Tate did let her clean house, mop the floors, make beds, help with the laundry, etc. Sort of like Cinderella on steroids, only worse.

Diana doesn't get the knight in shining armor or a glass slipper. Diana got Butch and his black 1959 Ford Falcon with all his shining glory, not armor.

Diana graduated from high school and started out on her own. Where to go, how to get there? Diana found an apartment with a young girl named Nita. The apartment was within walking distance of her employment. Nita hired with the State at the same time and same office as Diana. Cost of the apartment was seven dollars and fifty cents per week for each.

Butch took Diana shopping for flatware, purchased at S.S. Kresge, a place setting for four at a cost of eleven dollars and ninety-five cents, melmac dishes for four for nineteen dollars and ninety-five cents and pillows, sheets, and blankets, free from friends and relatives.

CHAPTER TWENTY-SEVEN

*** THE MARRIAGE ***

Within a few months Butch and Diana were married September 2, 1961 and Nita moved out and Ron moved in.

What a wedding! Unbelievable! The huge numbers that were there! Let's see there was Butch's mother and dad, Butch's brother Jack and his wife, Gary, Butch's best man, and Juanita, Diana's best friend and matron of honor. Of course the preacher, that about covers it. Cost of the wedding: preacher was ten dollars, which included cost of church and rehearsal, and dinner at local restaurant including tip was about eighty dollars. This was 1961, cost today maybe four hundred, tops!

The wedding march, "Here Comes the Bride" played on a forty-five RPM record player. Diana's mother couldn't or wouldn't come, although Butch's dad said he would pick her up and drive her to the wedding. Diana's sisters and brother were much too young to go on their own. Butch's dad picked up the bill, except for the ten dollar preacher, Butch got that. The marriage has lasted only fifty-three years to date. Butch says, "Only eight people at the wedding. Everyone I loved best. I wonder how long a ten thousand dollar wedding would last?"

*** LIFE IS GOOD ***

Married at one o'clock, reception at seven o'clock. Off on honeymoon at nine o'clock. Butch and Diana had saved a little over two hundred and fifty dollars for their honeymoon. Butch would put his change, and occasionally a dollar here, fifty cents there, in the safest place he knew, a two foot tall plastic coin bank in the shape of a white duck! Diana used the lesser safe place, the local bank.

Guess you can see who is going to pay bills and balance the checkbook in the future.

Paris look out! Maybe not, but they did head out for the five to six hour drive to Niagara Falls, Canada.

Butch is thinking just married, sex, honeymoon, sex, most beautiful girl in the world, sex, motel, sex.

Butch was one month under twenty and like most guys that age, as he puts it, hornier than a three-peckered billy goat.

Cross the Blue Water Bridge in Butch's almost new 1957 yellow and white Ford convertible. Butch put every penny he had into this car, all one thousand dollars. It was worth every penny.

Hair blowing in the breeze, not really. Remember Brylcreem? Terrific car, beautiful new wife, sex. Butch had a real difficult time thinking of more than one thing at a time.

Port Huron, cross the Blue Water Bridge to Sarnia, Canada, make a quick turn to the right, first motel on the right.

Butch said to the clerk, "Hello, I'd like a room."

"What kind?"

"One with a bed."

"No, I mean second floor? Overlooking the water?"

"I don't care as long as it has a bed," Butch said, "It can be a single bed if that's all you got."

"How old are you?" This is 1961, they asked questions like that back then, especially in Canada.

"Twenty next month."

"You don't look twenty."

Butch looked about sixteen, all five foot six, one hundred twenty pounds of him. He only shaved about twice a month. "I'll be twenty next month." Butch pulled out his Michigan driver license. Back then the only identification on the Michigan driver license was your birth date, color of eyes, color of hair, no picture.

"Why do you want a room?" asked the desk clerk.

"I just got married."

"Where's your wife?"

"In the car waiting for me to get a room with a bed."

"Do you have a marriage license?"

"Yes."

"Can I see it?"

Butch was thinking, "You got to be kidding! I can't stand here much longer in this condition, but if it gets me a room with a bed..." But instead he said, "I'll be right back."

Out to the car. "Diana, I need the marriage license and your driver license." Butch had just taught Diana how to drive before they got married. She got her driver's license out and gave them to Butch.

"What do you need my driver license for?" Diana asked.

"If I have to explain it to you we won't get a room for an hour," he told her.

Back to the motel.

Butch handed the marriage license to the clerk. "Here is the marriage license and my wife's driver license." The clerk looked at the license, looked at Butch, looked at the license, looked at Butch.

"Okay, that will be ten dollars. Nine dollars if you pay in U.S. dollars, ten if you pay in Canadian. I think the exchange is ten percent today. I expect you will be paying in U.S. and take advantage of the exchange?"

Butch looked the desk clerk straight in the eye and said, "All I want is a room with a bed."

Finally a room with a bed. Life is really great now. At least for Butch!

*** THE HONEY MOON ***

A couple of days at the falls. Yes, Butch and Diana actually saw the falls for a couple of minutes, then over to Buffalo on the United States side of the falls. They drove from Buffalo to the south end of Michigan, up the full length of the mitten part of Michigan to the Mackinac Bridge, across the straits of Mackinac to Mackinac Island, spent a day, drove back to the two room apartment in Corunna with a couple dollars left from the two hundred and fifty. Let's see you pull that off today!

CHAPTER TWENTY-EIGHT

*** STARTING ANEW ***

Monday morning. Starting a new life together. Diana set off to the Department of Social Service only five blocks away, which she walked every morning, home for lunch, and back again at five o'clock. She made a dollar sixty-five an hour with medical benefits that she had to pay part of and a retirement program she contributed to. Butch drove to work at his father's machine shop twenty miles away and made one hundred twenty-five dollars a week.

Butch and Diana both thought they had died and gone to heaven. During the next year things were as good as it was going to get in the machine shop business. Not really good, not really bad.

*** A BUNDLE FROM HEAVEN ***

On May 23, 1962 a bundle from heaven, SHERRI. Diana and

Butch's daughter is born.

They were not much more than children themselves. Diana had not yet turned nineteen and Butch was barely past twenty. Diana was the oldest among six siblings so she knew about changing diapers, etc. Butch was like an only child as his brother, Jack, was eleven years older.

Shortly after Diana and Butch were married, they purchased a mobile home, brand new, fifty five feet long, and ten feet wide. It had two bedrooms and cost forty-five hundred dollars. Butch had to have his father co-sign because he was not old enough. Back then twenty-one was legal age. Butch parked the mobile home behind the machine shop in Byron. There weren't many building ordinances in Byron at the time.

Diana loved having her own place and kept the place so clean and shiny. She cleaned the entire trailer a least once a week and polished all the paneled walls. Every time Butch would put out a cigarette in the ash tray, Diana would clean it. Sherri just sparkled, she was so clean. Butch finally had to tell Diana to let Sherri get dirty once in a while.

CHAPTER TWENTY-NINE

*** BLUE CHIP TO NO CHIP ***

All wasn't so great with the machine shop. Butch's dad and brother changed the name of the shop from Blue Chip to Diversified Enterprise, Inc. The name was changed but the business was doing poorly. Harold didn't know much about the business world. All he knew was hard work. He didn't know the difference between a debit and a credit and couldn't care less.

The shop did alright when it first started. Harold got most of the business from employers he had been employed by. Now he was working on a sub- sub- sub-contract basis. The slightly bigger job shops would give him the blueprints and say, "Here, make these parts for this much money."

When Harold moved to Byron he had to start paying for a bigger building, fixing things up, and hiring people. He just didn't have the know-how to bid on contracts. He knew how long it would take to make a part but he did not know how to factor in wages, social security, unemployment, cost of heat, electric, and so forth.

Little by little the shop was going into debt. When the bills came in, he wouldn't open them.

Harold got behind, he would make the payroll in cash and forget to put aside money to send to the government for payroll taxes. Once the shop got so far behind in paying the light bill, the light company shut off the power. Butch and the family spent the night in the dark. A friend of Butch's came to the door and knocked. Butch and his mother sat quietly until his friend left. They were too embarrassed to answer the door.

Jack started working in the shop right out of high school, and learned the trade. After a year or so, he was drafted into the Marines. This was in 1951 during the Korean War. Fortunately he did not have to go overseas. He spent the entire time at Paris Island, South Carolina, working in an office. Jack was very intelligent, and worked his way up fast in the Marines. He could handle the do-it-by-the-book routine. He could take orders and he could give them. In the military everything is written out, do this, do that, everything is black and white, no gray. Jack made the rank of buck sergeant, three striper, in eighteen months which was very fast.

Jack married a girl from Utley by the name of Lillian. She was a person who wanted more out of life than what she had at Utley. She was willing to work for it. Lillian worked at the P X on Paris Island while Jack was in the Marines. The P X is like a department store for service men.

When Jack got out of the service, Lillian obtained employment at General Motors. Jack and Lillian lived in a small house in Byron. They divorced after only five years of marriage.

The relationship between Jack and Harold was not good almost from the time Jack got home from the Marines. Harold really didn't care about money, or how much or how many hours he had to work to get it. He was happy if he had a newspaper to read and a T.V. to watch, food in his stomach and clothes on his back. The shop to him was not only the place he worked, but it also was his hobby. It took Butch years to figure this out. It was something Jack never understood.

Most people work to make money and work as little as possible to get it. This was the philosophy of most people including Jack and Butch. As you can guess, this was gas and a match together waiting for

153

a place to happen. The differences between Harold and Jack grew more and more each day.

Edna didn't help matters out. There was no secret that Edna and Harold didn't get along. Edna thought others had it better financially then she did. She might have been right, but it created problems between her and Harold. Harold said that Edna pitted Jack against him. Butch, in later years, was not sure that Harold wasn't right.

In 1960 Jack married for a second time to a woman named Betty. They had two girls, Jackie eleven months older than Janet. Jack, his wife, and two daughters, moved to California to start anew. Butch and Diana also moved to California, only to return to Michigan after about five weeks as Butch could not find work.

After returning home from California with a wife and child and two dollars fifty cents in his pocket and no job, Butch once again turned to his father for employment. Butch's main job in the shop was the bookkeeping, comprised of making out payroll, accounts receivable/payable, and purchasing. Butch would also help Harold bid jobs. Harold would tell him how long it would take to do the labor, and he would figure the material, tooling, overhead and other costs. A lot of responsibility for a guy barely over twenty years old.

This system seemed to work. Except when they didn't get a job they bid on. Harold thought Butch was too high on his part of the bid, but by and large, they got along very well. For a brief time the shop actually showed a profit. Then a steady decline. Butch finally realized that one or the other would have to go out on their own.

Butch was eager to try something new. After all, the machine shop was really his dad's business, not his.

CHAPTER THIRTY

*** BATTER UP!!! Summer 1964 Baseball in Hicksville***

Tom, a good friend of Butch's, was coaching his first year in little league. His son has just turned eight years old and was ready for his first year in baseball. Tom had helped another guy the year before, but he was now head coach of eight to twelve year old boys. Tom didn't have a clue what to do. He was one of the nicest guys you would ever want to know, but he never really played baseball. He was just trying to be a good father to his son.

Most of the coaches in Little League had sons playing. While their sons were playing they coached, when their sons left, the coaches left with them, and some other father with a first or second year player would become coach. This was Tom.

156

Tom asked, "Butch, how would you like to help me coach Little League this year?"

"Yeah sure, that would be great." Butch had played Little League baseball from age ten to sixteen and high school baseball for three years. He was an avid fan of the Detroit Tigers, and watched and listened to all their games.

Butch helped Tom one year then moved up and became head coach of his own twelve nose-picking, butt-scratching, spitting-between-the-teeth players. They were just average Joes, but Butch, now an old man of twenty-four, and his mighty twelve thought they were Mickey Mantles and Babe Ruths all rolled into one. Butch was the youngest head coach and the only one that didn't have a son playing. Butch's son, Cary, wasn't born until 1967.

Butch just loved baseball. Every night after work, down to the baseball field he went to practice. He looked at his team with pride. The field was a mess. It was the same field he played on as a teenager, all dirt, not a blade of grass anywhere. In place of grass were stones, a lot of stones. Every year at the beginning of the baseball season, all the ballplayers would line up across the diamond and pick up stones. By the

157

end of the year a new crop of stones would appear. It was just like the stones grew out of the ground.

Before any games were played, before the first practice, the Byron Little League coaches, assistant coaches, anyone interested in Little League would meet and go over rules and other important information. Most of the time these meetings were not well attended. This was not the fun part of Little League, this was the business part.

First organizational meeting three people showed up, Naomi, Ruth and Butch. The three were standing next to the phone booth under the stoplight in town. They were waiting to get into the building where the meeting was to be held. Finally, the president of the Little League and long time coach showed up. Paul asked, "Where's everybody?"

"Looks like we're it," Butch answered.

Paul, not a man long on patience, said, "That's it, I quit!" and handed a stack of papers to Butch. Paul turned, got into his car and drove off into the sunset. The three of them were speechless.

The women turned to Butch and asked, "What do we do?"

"The best we can. Let's start by electing officers."

"Elect officers?" Ruth asked, "There's just the three of us."

158

Butch said, "Well, that should make it easy. Who wants to be president?"

Naomi told him, "You do."

"I second the nomination," Ruth said.

"Alright, Naomi," Butch accepted the nomination and added, "You're the treasurer."

"I second," Ruth said again.

"Ruth, you're secretary."

"I second," Naomi said this time.

Two women who knew nothing about baseball and a guy that knew nothing about running a Little League of sixteen teams and over two hundred boys were now in charge of the fate of Byron Little League.

Butch said, "Find the checkbook and see how much money we have to work with. Here it is. Oh well, no problem with money, we have a whopping fifty one dollars and change."

"Well, the two of you take this list of last years' coaches, call them and ask if they are going to be coaches this year. If not, ask them if they know of someone that will take their team and contact them. We will have to set a date, time and place for our next meeting. Tell the coaches that we will be giving out the equipment for their teams the night of the meeting. If they or their assistant coach do not show, they will not be coaching this year," Butch said.

Ruth asked, "What if they get upset or have questions?"

"Tell them to call me."

"Where will we meet? Where is the equipment?" asked Naomi.

"Paul has all the equipment in his barn. I will clean out my garage and put the equipment there. We'll meet at the ball field at six thirty Tuesday, if that's alright with the two of you."

Naomi asked, "Where is the money going to come from?"

"According to deposits in the checkbook, the village, township and school donate money. We will start there," replied Butch.

At the Tuesday night meeting, Butch said, "Thanks for coming. At the organizational meeting the other night only Naomi, Ruth, Paul and myself showed. Paul said he was done and gave us the books. We held an election and voted me president, Naomi treasurer, and Ruth secretary. If any one of you want the jobs speak up, if not that's the way it will be this year."

160

Butch was told after the meeting someone said, "Who does he think he is? God? Naomi said to him, "No, more like Moses."

A few days later at the first practice, Butch was ready for the season. Well, not quite. During one of the practices, one of the parents came up to Butch and said, "They're having a meeting at the high school boardroom and they want you there."

"What for?" asked Butch.

"Something about Little League."

Butch entered the boardroom.

The high school principal said, "Have a seat. Something has come up about the use of tax payers' money. It boils down to this: the school, village, and the township will not be able to give tax money to the Little League anymore."

Butch inquired, "Why, they have in the past?"

"New law regarding tax money going from one tax base to another," was his answer.

Butch never really got a good explanation. Bottom line, there was no money for Little League.

The principal went on, "The village and township's hands are tied. The school, however, can help if they have complete control of the Little League. They can sponsor the Little League."

Butch looked around the room and saw a bunch of sad faces except the principal's smiling face.

Bob, representing the village said, "Butch, I really hate to see the Little League lose its independence, but I can see no other way."

Butch said, "Thanks, but no thanks, we'll find a way to raise our own money." He turned and walked out the door.

About the time Butch was out of the building, he realized he had no money and no way of raising money, two women that knew nothing about baseball, and a guy who knows nothing about running and financing a summer baseball program. It just gets better!

Back to the ball field after practice. Naomi and Ruth were walking toward Butch with smiling faces. "What's up?"

Butch answered, "The school, village, and township aren't giving us any money this year. Why? I really don't know. Some new law that was passed about tax money from one place going to another. I really don't know what to do."

The girls may not know much about baseball but they do know

about raising money.

"Well, I know when our church needs money they have raffles," Naomi offered.

Ruth affirmed, "Ours too."

Naomi and Ruth were both Catholics. Thank God for those money making Catholics!

Naomi went on, "We've both been involved in raffles."

"What do we do?" Butch asked.

Naomi said, "Get some business people to donate free prizes, put up fifty dollars in cash as a prize. Print the tickets, give each kid a handful for their parents to buy or sell. The guys that work in the factories are buying and selling tickets all the time."

So it went. Naomi also started selling candy and soft drinks at the games out of the back of her station wagon. At year's end, Byron Little League had more money than ever!

Butch also suggested, along with the raffle and the concession station wagon, to outfit the boys in T-shirts with business names on the back. Of course we charged for the advertisement.

The best thing that ever happened to Little League baseball in

Byron was when the school, village, and township wouldn't pay up.

Surprising what two women that knew nothing about baseball and a young guy that knew nothing about running a summer baseball program can do, and they did it without government help. Actually, they ran it better! To this day that is how the money is raised for Byron Little League Baseball.

Too bad there wasn't any plaques or recognition for those two ladies, Naomi and Ruth, so people would know who saved their program forty-five plus years ago. Both Naomi and Ruth are in heaven now, probably running raffles and selling candy out of the back of their chariots. No one knows all they did. Butch does. Thanks, Naomi and Ruth. Thank God you were Catholics.

CHAPTER THIRTY-ONE

*** IT'S A BOY! ***

In 1967 two very important things happened. Another bundle from heaven, this time a boy named CARY. Sherri was now five, starting kindergarten in the fall.

The second big event of that year was Butch entering the world of work outside of family employment. Butch was now twenty-five years old. The one thing he knew is he didn't want to work in manufacturing anymore. Maybe sales. He was always a good talker and liked people.

Butch read the want ads in the newspaper and saw an ad by an employment agency. He knew a little about employment agencies. The agency would get job listings from employers and run ads in the newspaper, interview applicants, and then send them to the employer. If someone got hired they paid the agency a fee. Sometimes the employer paid the fee if the job was hard to fill.

One of the first jobs Butch interviewed with the agency for was a sales job to sell cigarettes to supermarkets. Butch was a smoker then. He didn't smoke the brand of cigarettes the company was hiring for, and needless to say he wasn't hired.

Next, the agency sent Butch to interview with Keebler Biscuit Companies. (Biscuit companies are better known as cookie and cracker companies). Keebler was a new corporation. It purchased or merged with three or four other companies around the country to form one of the larger biscuit companies. The big boys on the block in the biscuit business were Nabisco, short for National Biscuit Company, and the Sunshine Bakeries. Butch interviewed with a man by the name of Bob Bigelow who was known in the Flint area as king of the soft sell.

Every industry had its top people and Bob was it in the biscuit industry. Bob was around fifty-five years old, about the same size and height as Butch, maybe slightly heavier. He dressed well and always wore his little black fedora which set him apart from most. Bob was the district manager for Keebler. The district covered most of southeast Michigan, which included Flint.

The interview was going well when Bob got a phone call.
The call was from a newly hired assistant sales manager named Kevin Ely. He was in his early thirties and over six feet tall. Kevin was from the Columbus, Ohio area.

The phone call went something like this. The phone rang, Bob answered, "Hello. Oh, hi, Kevin. Yes, I'm interviewing a good candidate right now. Looks like me when I was younger. Yes, about my size. No he won't have trouble stocking the top shelves."

Good thing Kevin wasn't holding the interview. Butch got the job and Kevin trained him. He and Kevin hit it off well. Butch was eager to do well and worked hard. The job mainly consisted of selling displays that fit on the ends of supermarket aisles and some free standing displays. He also had to order merchandise to restock shelves. The job was right down his alley. The pay was fair, one hundred twenty-five dollars a week, the same as his dad paid him plus he got a car to drive on his territory. He could use the car for his own use, all he had to do is pay for the gas.

The merchandise was delivered by truck. In the big stores that had union contracts, the store employees put the merchandise on the displays and shelves. In smaller ma and pa stores, the sales people had to put up the stock.

Butch learned a great deal about the retail business, like rotating stock to keep it fresh, a penny increase meant big profits when that penny was on thousands of pieces of merchandise. He was surprised to find out how much money his cookies and crackers brought in. In one store one week's average sales was more than seven hundred fifty dollars. Today that would probably be five times as much.

If a company would give a store a TPR, temporary price reduction, it could sell an end display or a stand alone display worth hundreds of dollars. Sometimes the TPR was just one or two cents a package off.

Trying to get the attention of a store manager was something else. Managers had little time or love for sales people. You usually had to talk to them on the run and you had maybe one or two minutes to make your pitch.

Butch was a good sales person. When the company made some cutbacks, Bob had to let one of the sales people go. Butch had the least seniority but Bob let someone else go. There wasn't a union in the biscuit business. You produced or you were out. After a while the company decided to weed out the older managers and bring in new blood. They let Bob go. This was very upsetting to the company's sales team in Flint.

Butch had already decided to look for other employment and had interviewed with a life insurance company. He had not been officially hired by the life insurance company when he was called in to meet the new district sales manager from Keebler.

The new guy was a college boy and we do mean boy. Twenty-four years old, with no experience in the food sales business. The new Keebler manager had less than nice things to say about Bob. Butch got hot and told him he could stick the job "where the sun don't shine".

When Butch started on the drive home from the meeting he realized two things. He didn't have a job, but he did have a wife and two kids. Lesson learned: Don't leave one job until you know you have another. Butch had to go home and try to explain to Diana how stupid he was.

As for Bob Bigelow, he was hired back within two months and retired two years later.

169

All turned out well. Butch got a job at a life insurance company. First, he had to study for an exam to pass the state insurance test. Lucky for Butch he passed. If he didn't he was done, no job, no unemployment. There weren't unemployment benefits when you quit a job without good cause. Telling the company to stick it doesn't meet the criteria for good cause.

CHAPTER THIRTY- TWO

*** FIRST HOME SWEET HOME ***

During this time Diana and Butch purchased a nice double corner lot just two blocks away from the shop building. They a paid a whopping one thousand dollars. Diana and Butch didn't have any money to speak of.

They bought a Capp Home to put on the lot. Capp Homes was a company out of Minnesota that sold pre-cut homes of very nice quality material. The home came complete with all building materials, plumbing, furnace package, cupboards, everything. All you had to have was a lot, a job and good credit. Butch and Diana's credit was very good.

They made an appointment at the local bank, the same bank that Harold and Butch had been banking with for several years. The branch manager wouldn't give Butch the time of day, saying he couldn't loan money on a vacant lot.

Butch couldn't believe it! After all the years Harold and the shop had banked with them, not to mention Butch owned the lot and had a house and materials for collateral. There had been one or two issues with the bank in the past.

A few years back Harold wanted to borrow money to buy a lathe for the shop. He just couldn't seem to make the bank manager, a guy named Mel, see the value of the loan. Mel just didn't understand machinery or the manufacturing business. Byron was a farm town. They knew farming, that was it. Mel started hemming and hawing around. "I don't know Harold, what would I do with a lathe if you weren't able to pay the loan?"

Harold explained, "Mel, look at the lathe as if it were a cow, only it won't die!"

Butch didn't think Mel saw all the humor in the statement but Mel did give Harold the loan.

After a few more dealings with Mel and the bank, Harold transferred his banking account to another bank.

Butch felt that might have been a factor in Mel's attitude about lending him money to build a house. Nevertheless, Butch and Diana got the Capp Home delivered. Capp Homes financed the construction for up to six years. After that time they had to refinance.

Butch continued working for the life insurance company and everything was going okay. Of course, Diana was the mainstay and was still working for the Department of Social Services.

The building of the house was going very slow. Butch was less of a carpenter than he was a machinist. He did know how to contract out the work and get bids, find carpenters that would scab contract, work on their own after hours and on weekends from their regular jobs. Fortunately for Butch, there was a big brick and block union strike. He got his basement blocks and fireplace built for nearly half price. He also knew people in the drywall business. Remember Skeeter? Skeeter and his brother-in-law hung drywall for a living. Skeeter's brother-in-law also helped Butch with the plumbing. Another friend knew a guy that was a former heating and cooling guy. He put in all the duct work and furnace for Butch.

Butch and Diana had been living in the house for about five years. The house was eighteen hundred square feet, three bedrooms, one and a half baths, one car garage, set on two tree lined corner lots. Time was running out on the refinancing.

Butch told Diana there shouldn't be any problem getting

refinancing as they owed less than eight thousand dollars. Once again, Butch approached the local bank for refinancing. Mel, the same guy that wouldn't lend Butch money five years ago, hadn't changed much.

When Butch set out the details for the loan, Mel's answer was short and sweet. He smiled and said, "We don't do that type of financing."

Butch heard of a bank in Corunna that was doing a lot of home loans. He made an appointment with the branch manager, a man named Clare. Butch told Diana they had better sit close to the door so they wouldn't have far to throw them out.

Clare was a professional looking man with pure white hair. Butch explained the situation. Clare said, "Let me take a drive over to Byron and take a look."

Two or three hours later, Clare called, "No problem, come over tomorrow and sign the papers."

Things were looking up for Butch and Diana.

BUTCH

CHAPTER THIRTY-THREE

*** LIFE IS GOOD, NOT FOR LONG ***

In the spring of 1968 the family, Edna, Butch, and Diana started noticing a change in Harold. He seemed to tire out faster and had a difficult time going up and down the stairs. He seemed to need more sleep. Butch finally convinced Harold to go to the doctor. The doctor said Harold had Hodgkin's Disease. Actually, Harold had lung cancer.

The doctor that Harold went to knew how much the word cancer scared Harold so the doctor called it Hodgkin's Disease. The condition was terminal. As time went by Harold's condition got worse. The business was failing miserably. Jack had left some years before and was living in California. Butch was working as a life insurance salesman and helping Harold with the office work.

Harold decided to try to sell the shop. There wasn't much of a market for such a small machine shop. He did have a patent on a tool for the replacement of mufflers but the market was fading out.

The only person that showed any interest in buying the shop was a young man named Larry from a nearby town. Larry became

175

known as Larry the Liar. He couldn't tell the truth, even if it sounded better. Larry was in his early thirties and operated a very small shop with a few rundown machines. He was one of those guys who tried to make everybody think he was a genius. He really didn't have much of an education or a whole lot of talent. What he did have was a whole lot of BS. Butch's dad was desperate and sold the shop with no money down and a hope to pay.

Larry said Harold could stay on as long as he wanted and Larry would pay him. Larry paid no one. He didn't pay the insurance for the men that worked for him, and he didn't pay heat, lights, taxes, or any bills. He just took.

By January of 1969 Harold could not work anymore and Larry wasn't paying him. In late March and early April of 1969 Butch and Diana noticed that Edna was acting strange. She seemed to lose her balance a little. She had to use both hands to drink her coffee. She seemed out of it. Early to mid April Edna's speech started to slur.

Butch and Diana took her to the doctor. The doctor referred Edna to the Henry Ford Hospital in Detroit. When Butch took his mother to Henry Ford, she was moving very slowly. She was only fifty

-seven years old.

After two weeks with Edna was in Henry Ford, the doctors asked to speak with Butch and Diana. They said that Edna had blocked carotid arteries and there was nothing they could do. Nowadays there is a relatively simple operation that Butch calls roto-rootering the arteries and you go on living for years. Not so in 1969.

Harold was in the University of Michigan Hospital in Ann Arbor the past two weeks dying of lung cancer.

Butch now had his father in the University of Michigan Hospital in Ann Arbor and his mother at Henry Ford Hospital in Detroit, a job in Shiawassee County, a wife, and two small children. Butch was only twenty-seven. No one to help. Butch's brother Jack was still living in California.

When Butch and Diana brought Edna home from the hospital, she could not stand. She could not control her hands or her head. Her head would just flop from one side to the other. When Butch got Edna to the car he had to lift her from the wheel chair into the back seat of his Volkswagen. Butch, with Diana's help, could barely lift her in. He could not understand a word when Edna tried to talk. They were

177

somehow able to get Edna up the flight of stairs to the second floor apartment back in Byron. Within a few days Butch borrowed a hospital bed from a relative and put it in the living room.

Edna could barely swallow. She had no control of her kidneys or bowels. Diana had to clean her up several times a day. The stress and work was was taking a toll on both Diana and Butch.

Years later, Butch said Diana and he looked like death eating a cracker. Butch and Diana's weight was the same, one hundred two pounds.

While driving to sell insurance, Butch started to feel his heart beat fast. He became short of breath and started sweating. What Butch was having was a panic attack. He thought he was having a heart attack. The condition with Harold in the hospital and Edna home having to have twenty-four hour care was getting to be too much.

Butch called for an ambulance to take Edna to the local hospital. The emergency room doctor said there was nothing he could do, that Butch would have to take his mother to a nursing home. He didn't have any money and knew nothing about getting any help. He simply turned to the doctor with tears in his eyes and said, "She's yours," and turned and started walking out of the hospital.

The doctor said, "Wait a minute. I'll admit your mother until we can find some place for her, but she can't stay here long."

On May thirteenth, fourteen days before her fifty-eighth birthday, Edna took care of staying in the hospital too long. She simply passed away.

Butch asked the doctor, "What do we do now?"

He said, "You need to have someone from a funeral home pick your mother up. They will take it from there."

Butch called Lewis Small of the Lewis N. Small mortuary in Byron. The next day Butch and Diana met with Lewie in the office of the mortuary.

After the I'm sorry, how are you doing?" small talk took place, they got down to business.

Lewie asked, "Butch, do you have a burial site?"

"No."

"Do you want your mother buried in the local cemetery?"

"Yes."

"I will take you and Diana there later and pick out a nice site.

You will have to pick out a casket, you know. We have them here if you would like to view them. In order for me to help you, you need to tell me how much life insurance your mother has."

"None. Ma had so many problems over the years she was not insurable. Dad has twenty-five hundred dollars but..."

Lewie interrupted, "I know." This being a very small town and Harold and Butch were well known, so everybody knew that both Harold and Edna were in bad health.

"I think we can do a very respectful funeral for both with that amount of insurance," Lewie said. Twenty-five hundred dollars isn't a lot of money, but in 1969 it was worth in today's money twelve to fifteen thousand. Remember gas was only thirty-five cents a gallon.

Butch didn't really know Lewie that well but found out he was one of the nicest people he would come across.

Into the casket room.

Butch has said since, "Don't make anyone go through picking out a casket, pick out your own ahead of time".

Lewie picked out a casket and said, "Butch, here is a very nice one for your mother." It was a light mint green.

Butch said, "What do you think, Diana?"

"It looks beautiful," she said.

Butch asked, "Lewie, do you mind if we pick one out for my dad? You know it is just a matter of a short time."

"That sounds good. Here is a nice steel gray. Looks right for your dad."

"Okay."

Between visiting his father in Ann Arbor and preparing for his mother's funeral, Butch and Diana were very busy. Butch's brother came back for his mother's funeral, then went back to California. On May the nineteenth Butch's dad passed away.

This time Butch was a little more prepared. Harold would be buried next to Edna, the casket was already picked out, and both funerals were paid for. Jack came home for Harold's funeral and returned to California.

*** LARRY THE LIAR ***

The fight with Larry the Liar over the shop wasn't over. It had just begun. Larry finally walked away from the shop, the electricity had been turned off, there wasn't any heat in the building, some of the water pipes had burst, the insurance on the building was not paid, the real estate tax was overdue and the building was being put up for tax sale. Butch didn't have the money to pay for any of the bills.

Butch made an appointment with the bank to see if he could borrow enough money to pay all the bills and do necessary repairs to bring the building presentable for sale.

The bank holding the mortgage on the building was, you got it, the same bank that wouldn't lend Butch money to build his house. The same bank, a different person, same mindset. His name was Joe. Joe was a big time farmer who also ran the bank.

Joe said, you're right again, "No." They would not refinance the building, let alone give extra money to repair the building or pay off back taxes and insurance.

Butch said, "Well, I'll find some other bank."

Joe, with a half laugh, said, "You won't find anyone to lend you money on that building in its current condition."

Thanks Joe.

Butch remembered Clare at the bank in Corunna.

"Diana, we need to see if Clare will lend us the money. We need to sit a lot closer to the door this time." The situation was a lot different. Butch had a very old building in need of repair, money owed against it, back taxes, and insurance. The likelihood of renting or selling the building after repair was not good.

Butch said to Diana, "Even if we get the money to repair the building and pay off the bills, I still don't have the money to make the new mortgage payment until we sell the building. Who knows how long that will be?"

Then with a half-hearted laugh and smile Butch said, "Diana, this is what we're going to do. We're going to ask Clare for all the money it takes to pay off the mortgage, back taxes, other bills, repair costs and enough money to pay the new mortgage for a year, one month at a time." In essence use the bank's money to pay the bank payments. Sure, no problem. Clare would buy into that!

"Do you really believe he will?" asked Diana.

Butch answered, "Of course not! If he will buy part of it, he will buy into it all!"

The total cost was not that much money. If the building was in repair, the question of refinancing would have been easy. The question was, would Clare believe that Butch could manage everything, including selling the building?

Butch made the call to Clare. "Hello, this is Butch over in Byron. Do you remember me? You loaned Diana and I money to build our first house. It was a year ago."

"Yes, how are you and Diana doing?"

"Just fine," Butch said. "I have another need for a loan."

"What is it?"

Butch, after a long pause, said, "Well, I have a building in town that I inherited from my parents. It was used as my father's machine shop and has two apartments on the second floor. I'm wanting to sell it, but it needs some fixing up and I need to pay off the existing mortgage. I would like to come talk with you if I could."

"Let's see. What about two o'clock?"

Surprised, Butch said, "Two today?"

"Yes, if that's okay with you."

Butch, "I'll be there."

At two o'clock Butch and Diana entered the bank. Clare smiled and motioned for them to come into his office.

"Have a seat." The smile left Clare's face for a moment, then came back. "Tell me what you're looking for, how much, and your plans for selling the property."

As Butch looked back on that moment when the smile left Clare's face and returned, it must have been when Clare got a close look at the two of them. He must have wondered, "What the hell had happened to these two kids? They look skinny, pale, and worried."

Butch was so skinny his face looked all nose and ears. His cheeks were sunken in. Diana was not much better.

Butch started, "It's this way, I can't lie to you, the building is in need of repair. I owe back taxes. I need money to pay off the existing mortgage and some other small bills. I need fifteen thousand dollars." This amount included the money Butch would use to pay the new mortgage.

Clare listened and said, "Let me and one of my associates drive over to Byron and take a look at your building. Do you have a key?"

"Sure, here it is. "

Clare told him, "I'll call you later this afternoon."

Butch and Diana got in the car and drove home. On the way,

185

Butch was so nervous that he almost broke down in tears. Everything was riding on Clare and the bank. Without the loan they would lose the building and the machinery in the building. They would lose everything. All of Harold's hard work and dreams would be for nothing, all because of that asshole at that Farmer's Bank.

The loan was approved!

Butch was able to pay off the mortgage, the back taxes, repair the building and even make monthly payments back to the bank. Eventually the building was sold for a nice profit, which Butch and his brother shared.

If Clare's bank would not have made the loan, Butch believed that his father's conspiracy theory about the Farmer's Bank would have happened to them. During this time a lot of small farmers were going out of business, being auctioned off. As the farms were being auctioned off, the farmer and his family would stand around while the auctioneer sold their farm, their equipment, their livestock, their dreams. Everything down the drain. Of course the bank doing the foreclosure and auction was, you guessed it, the Farmer's Bank. Who was the clerk at the auction, the person handling the money? Right again, good ole

Joe, manager of the Farmer's Bank.

Harold said the bank would lend the farmer just a little less than they needed to make a go of it. If the farmer stubbed his toe and didn't get enough money for their crops or livestock, the bank got the farm and all that went with it. The bank then resold the equipment and farm for more than was owed. Harold also believed some of that money found its way into some of the bankers' pockets. We won't say who but their initials are J-O-E.

Butch felt this was exactly what would happen with the shop. He wouldn't be able to pay the debt on the shop, the bank would foreclose, and sell everything at a profit. There was no way to know if Harold's conspiracy theory would proven true for the shop, but it sure looked like he was right about the farmers.

It just happened that a guy named Audest from a nearby town was interested in buying the shop and patent. He was a man in his late fifties or sixties, small built, and had a very pronounced limp. Audest was never married. His main occupation was buying and selling land contracts.

Audest also owned a restaurant called Lou Mars. Lou Mars was one of those twenty-four hours, seven days a week places. Young people hung out there. As a matter of fact, when Butch was a teenager he and some of his cronies hung out at Lou Mars. Butch knew Audest from those days.

About the time of Harold's death, Butch noticed a strange relationship forming, a sort of triangle developing between Audest, Joe the bank manager, and Larry the Liar. Audest was often at the auctions the Farmer's Bank held. He and Joe seemed to be quite friendly with each other.

Audest knew Larry through Larry's machine shop. A real threesome was forming. Again no real proof of conspiracy, no grassy knoll, if you know what I mean.

Butch and Jack had to take Larry to court to finally get the shop back and pay the bank every penny that was owed plus interest. No one ever lost a cent from the dealings with Harold's machine shop. Audest bought the machinery and patent from Butch and Jack. Audest then moved the machinery to Larry the Liar's place.

As far as Butch knows, Larry the Liar is still alive, living in a rundown house trailer suffering from arthritis. He looks older than his years and has long gray-white hair. He looks like something left over from the 1960 hippie era.

About ten or twelve years ago, Larry the Liar raised his ugly head once more. One evening Larry and one of his old cronies from the past were visiting. Somehow the talk turned to a heated discussion, then to a full blown argument. Larry told the crony to leave. When he didn't, Larry left the room and returned with a rifle. He pointed it at the guy who, at that moment, grabbed the end of the barrel. The gun went off killing the crony. Anyway, this is what Larry the Liar stated at his murder trial. Wouldn't you know it, the jury bought his story and Larry the Liar was set free.

Just about the time Butch refinanced the building, his brother Jack moved back from California. Butch really needed Jack. Jack was the stronger willed of the two. Jack, being a former Marine, had a very aggressive no compromise attitude which made selling the building and patent difficult. Regardless, Butch believed the sale would not have gone as well as it did with out Jack.

Maybe life would get better, maybe not.

189

CHAPTER THIRTY-FOUR

*** ONE THING AFTER ANOTHER ***

Right in the middle of all the confusion, Jack's daughter had an accident. She was riding her bicycle, fell and hit her head. She rode her bike home. The injury didn't look serious. She lay down an hour or so. Later, when Jack got home from work, his daughter woke up dazed and didn't know where she was. Jack called an ambulance and rushed her to the hospital.

The doctors discovered she had a blood clot on her brain. She became paralyzed on her left side, which affected the use of both her left arm and left leg for the rest of her life. She did marry and had two children.

All are working. Jack's working, Diana is working, Butch is working. All was well.... Maybe not.

No. Butch's nerves were shot. During the past few years Butch's overall physical health was good, but his emotional health, not so good. Butch believed the cause of the boils that broke out on his body was due to emotional stress that was throwing his body chemistry

190

out of whack.

Butch felt a change of jobs from insurance sales, which in itself was stressful, was needed. Butch really liked the insurance business but wanted something that had steady income, not commission sales.

What he really wanted was an independent insurance agency of his own. Although it was still selling insurance, homeowners and auto insurance was better than selling life insurance only.

It was not easy to start an independent agency. You had to find an insurance company willing to underwrite your business. The usual way of getting an agency is to purchase an existing agency. Butch was broke, no money.

Butch found a way. Working as an underwriter he would learn all the ins and outs of the insurance business, and make a decent pay at the same time. He landed a job with an insurance company and started work. He was trained by a young man named Bill. He learned a great deal about automobile and homeowners insurance from Bill.

Butch also learned that Bill was being paid less money than he was. Bill had been an employee of the company for over seven years. So much for company loyalty!

191

Everything seemed to be going well. Butch met a guy, Steven, who owned a real estate company in the town he and Diana lived in. Butch believed that insurance and real estate would be the best of both worlds.

Butch joined Steven, but found he really didn't like the real estate business. He said if you listed the property for sale and found a buyer, you had to represent both the buyer and the seller. It puts the sales person in a real bind.

The real estate company was too small to support one person, let alone two. Steven, who was going to help build the business, was busy making bigger deals in Lansing, which led to the business going under. Bad decision on Butch's part for leaving the underwriting job. Out of work again.

CHAPTER THIRTY-FIVE

*** BROTHER JACK TO THE RESCUE ***

Jack got a job at a small manufacturing company called Swartz.
The company was a new business started by three men in their late
forties to early fifties. Dave was the money guy and business brains of
the outfit. Lee was the machinist and plant operation manager and had
some money, and Leo was an engineer with no money but had THE
PRODUCT.

The product was a part of the carburetor system of an
automobile. The vacuum regulator, as it was called, was a small part not
weighing more than five or six ounces and was comprised of several
parts. Assembling the vacuum regulator was quite labor intensive.

The new company had its growing pains. It went from forty
employees to over two hundred in about a year and a half. Jack
mentioned to Butch that they were looking for someone to help in the
receiving inspection department. Butch, not being a machinist or having
the experience, questioned whether he would have the ability to do the
job. Jack said it would be a piece of cake.

Jack, "You can read mics (micrometers are used in the measuring of items in manufacturing). You can read simple blueprints. You'll be okay."

Butch still wasn't confident that he would be able to do the job so Butch asked Jack to go over reading mics and blueprints with him. Jack did and said, "Don't worry."

Jack talked to the supervisor of quality control and lined up the interview. Butch met with Ed, the QC supervisor. Ed was very laid back, easy going.

The company wanted to hire anyone with manufacturing experience. Come to find out, Butch was one of the more knowledgeable and experienced people there!

Butch started working in the receiving inspection department. He worked third shift, from eleven P.M. to seven to A.M. The shipping and receiving area was cold in the winter and hot in the summer. The big overhead doors were going up and down all the time. The little inspection room that Jack and Butch worked in only had a small electric space heater and no air conditioning in the summer.

Butch liked the work, hated the shift, wasn't wild about the conditions. Butch asked Ed when he was hired how long he would have to work third shift. Ed said, "About a month, then we'll put you on the floor inspecting parts as they are being assembled." First shift, inside, better pay. One month turned into two, then three, then four.

Finally, Ed called Butch into his office and said, "If you want, you can start in the WHITE ROOM on Monday, twenty cents an hour raise. Twenty cents on top of the three dollars and fifty cents." Now we're getting somewhere.

The WHITE ROOM was a special area set aside for final inspection of the vacuum regulator. The area was kept very clean, well lighted, temperature and humidity controlled.

Things were really going well. Butch was working a job that he liked and believed had a future. Diana was working. Jack was home and working. Life was good again. Well, of course, not for long.

Butch's brother was a very intelligent person with a great deal of experience in quality control. What he wasn't, was a person with patience. The company had hired several supervisors who were supposed to be experts in their field. Jack thought it was his obligation to let them know they weren't. Push came to shove between Jack and

195

management. When that happens the boss wins, whether the boss was right or wrong. Ed didn't disagree with Jack, he just didn't know what he wanted. Jack didn't like the way things were going.

Soon Jack found another job at a company called XXO Corp, which was a high profile corporation and had several divisions around the country. The plant manufactured special machinery. Almost everyone who worked at XXO were semi-skilled to highly skilled workers. Jack fit in perfectly.

Jack was very happy and encouraged Butch to hire into XXO. It was a growing company that had been around a long time. The problem was that Butch didn't have nearly the skill level needed. The XXO plant was growing faster than the rest of the brother and sister corporations. They needed help at all levels. Jack asked around and found out XXO was looking for someone in the production control and processing departments at entry level position, someone with some knowledge of blueprints and machining. That would be Butch.

Butch interviewed for and got the job. Butch felt great making twenty-five cents an hour more than at his last job. He would be mainly working in the office, wearing a tie to work. Great!

196

Butch's job was what they called a gofer. Not the animal. A gofer is a person who goes for this or goes for that. Go for. Get it?

Butch didn't care what they called him, he had a good paying job working in an office.

Being a gofer met technically you would need an education level of at least a kindergartner, well, maybe third grade. Third grade wasn't Butch's best. Remember?

Engineering would send down hundreds of blueprints. Most of the blueprints were large and had several different parts on each sheet. Butch's job was to cut each individual part out of the master blueprint and give them to the real production control guys.

Yes, guys. The only women working in manufacturing in the early to mid 1970s were clerical. What a waste of talent.

Looking back, Butch doesn't know how the talented women could stand running for coffee and saying "Here's your coffee, sir." Any woman could have done Butch's job. Lucky for him they didn't.

Another of Butch's jobs was to take the process sheet out to the machine area and give them to the foremen (supervisors). Most of the time the foremen would tell Butch, "Why don't you take it straight to the machinist?" That was fine with Butch. It got him out of the office and gave him a chance to talk with Jack and some of the other machinists.

Butch kind of liked the sounds and smells of lathes and mills working. He also learned a lot from the machinists about the different kinds of machines and what they did. The machinists seemed to like Butch and knew his brother was "one of them". The guys working in the plant, the machinists, didn't really care for the boys in the office, called the "shirts".

Most of the people working in production control and processing didn't have a lot of machining experience. They came from drafting and engineering, mainly paperwork guys.

When something went wrong in the production control area, no one in manufacturing would step up and say, "Can I help you?" However, because of Butch's machinest background they knew he was one of them.

Every once in a while Butch would buy the machinists a cup of coffee and shoot the bull with them. Ole Butch may have been smarter than we think!

After a few weeks of cutting up blueprints like paper dolls and running all over the plant delivering process sheets and messages, Butch overheard Larry, his boss, talking with a couple other guys about the time it was taking to type out the tapes for the 4K devlege and Bob Cat. The 4K devlege was a very large tape driven milling machine and the Bob Cat was just a smaller version.

Larry was a man in his late forties, very mild tempered. He looked older than his years. He wasn't well educated but was one of those people that had a lot of hands on experience. Larry was saying that it was just taking too long to make the tapes, that he might have to train one of the clerical girls to do the typing, but the girls didn't know anything about machining.

Milt, Larry's boss, a sixtyish, big, loud, rough, gruff German man said, "They might be able to type, but they wouldn't know if .250 of an inch was a foot or a mile. That could be trouble."

Butch piped up, "I type."

"What?"

Butch repeated, "I can type."

"Can you really type or are you a hunt and pecker?"

199

"No, I can type. I had two years of typing in high school and one year in college. At one time I could type fifty-five words per minute. I'm a little rusty."

Milt asked, "Larry, where the hell's he been? Get him on it."

The typewriter had a special attachment on the side. This attachment held a ribbon of paper on a spool. When you put a piece of paper in the typewriter and typed a word or letter, a hole was punched in the tape. This typewriter ribbon hole puncher was the first of what would be known later as CNC Machines (Computer Numerical Control). Whahoo! If Butch only knew then what he was really doing! Oh well. With Butch's ability to type and knowing how to read blue-prints he actually performed two jobs at once.

Before Butch started making the tapes, a lot of mistakes were made during the typing process because the production control guys were very poor typists. Quite often the tape had to be made over, which cost time. Time is money. Butch was making $4.25 an hour now. How much he saved them would be several times what XXO paid him.

Before long Butch was programing the most complicated blueprints. When he couldn't quite see where he was going on the blue print he would go out in the machining area and talk with the machine operator.

As we said before, the machinists all liked Butch, even more now for all the time and effort he saved them.

Live is good. Butch has got the best job he'd ever had. Lots of room for advancement!

Laid off! What the hell do you mean, laid off? How long? Will I be called back? What went wrong?

It seemed as though XXO Corporation was doing well, however, the XXO plant that Butch worked in, not so well. The specialty machines that XXO made were getting some competition from the Japanese. Add poor management to the equation, you get disaster.

The plant manager, Don, was a big guy about six foot five, two hundred fifty pounds. Don had a very loud mouth and very little talent.

Jack had a theory about bosses and people in higher positions. It went something like this. To be a boss, you had to be the owner's son, marry the owner's daughter or kiss a lot of butts. If that theory is correct, Don's brother must have been chairman of the board of directors, married the chairman of the board's daughter, and kissed

every butt of every stockholder. Let's say Don didn't have a very good

track record. What happens in a lot of large corporations is once a

person is promoted they just keep getting promoted, or at least moved

from one plant to another hoping the new plant can absorb their

incompetency. Apparently that was what XXO was trying to do with

Don.

Butch was told that he wouldn't be laid off long, a couple

weeks or so, go home and draw some rocking chair money

(unemployment insurance), take it easy. The layoff notice was given by

a guy named Joe, the manufacturing manager, in charge of all plant

operations.

Joe was in his early forties, short, medium built, and German,

very German. Joe was born in Germany in the mid-1930s. Joe was one

of those kids you saw in the news reels dressed in dark brown short

pants, light brown shirt, black belt, a black strap attached in front,

crossed over the shoulder attached in back, black shoes, dark brown

stockings. One of Hitler's little boys. Joe's mother, father, and two older

brothers, escaped from Germany when he was very young. He was so young he really didn't get indoctrinated to Nazism. Joe did rule the plant with an iron fist, very much like you would think a Nazi boss would. He was, if nothing else, very fair, but he did demand perfection.

Joe could take a joke. Every Friday all the male office personnel, would dress in dark brown pants, light brown shirt, dark brown tie. The first time the guys did this and Joe walked in, they didn't know what he would do. All he did was laugh, something he seldom did.

Normally Butch would have gotten his layoff notice from his supervisor, Larry. Joe liked Butch and thought he would do well for the corporation and thought the notice would be better if it came from him.

Joe was right. A couple weeks and Butch was back at work. Couple weeks later Butch was laid off again. The company only called him to catch up on tapes for the shop.

CHAPTER THIRTY-SIX

*** ANOTHER JOB ***

There had been a lot of shop gossip that work was slowing down. Butch had mentioned this to Diana. She suggested that he get a state job. Diana had been working for the Department of Social Service for also most fifteen years. It was 1975 now. Butch said okay.

Diana got copies of job bulletins listing state job openings, locations, and the qualifications.

Butch didn't realize the more locations you were willing to go to, the better chance of getting a job. He put down only Shiawassee County. Not much chance there. Department of Social Service, Secretary of State, State Police, Michigan Employment Security Commission were the only state offices in Shiawassee County, all small offices that had little turn over.

What do you know, an opening at the Michigan Employment Security Commission! Sounded good to Butch. He filled out an application. A few days later he got a letter of rejection. The letter stated that Butch didn't meet the minimum education level of four years of college or four years equivalent experience. Butch looked the state jobs bulletin over and decided to write an appeal.

Butch wrote that he had two years of college and over three years of life insurance sales. He stated that to sell life insurance one had to interview applicants to determine eligibility to issue policies based on insurance laws, rules, and regulations. Within a few days of Butch's appeal he received a notice to take the unemployment/employment interviewer test. He passed the test and was put on a register, which was a list of candidates to be interviewed.

Now all Butch had to do was wait for the call.

A couple weeks passed and bingo! Butch got the phone call from the manager of the Shiawassee office of the MESC, better known as the 'unemployment office'. Butch was presently collecting unemployment from that very office.

Butch's interview was with Ned Fibure. Ned was a barrel chested gruff ex-navy man.

After the interview Ned said, "You're not black." That was the proper term for African American in 1976.

Butch said, "No."

"On the form you filled out you stated you were black."

"Must have made a mistake."

"I have two openings. One for UI, the other is in ES." In state government you talked using letters instead of words, UI is unemployment insurance, and ES is employment service. "I have another interview in a few minutes with a women who says she is Indian, native American. If I hire her and put her in UI, I will be able to hire you for ES."

This was a time in the United States that government was trying to correct a lot of unjust hiring, housing, and other areas based on color, national origin. To correct the system and make it just for some, it made it unjust for others. The term was reverse discrimination. There is nothing right about discrimination, reverse or otherwise.

Butch returned home from the interview. He really didn't know what to think about Affirmative Action. All Butch knew was he didn't get the job. He still had his job at XXO. And who knows, maybe work would pick up. Sure enough, he went back to work for a couple of weeks.

Phone call from Ned.

"Ned Fibure here."

Butch beat him to the punch, "I'm no blacker than I was two weeks ago."

Ned laughed, "No, its okay, I was able to hire the woman for UI. I would like you to start as soon as you can. When would that be?"

"Let's see. Today is Tuesday. How about week from this coming Monday?" That's almost two weeks' notice, two weeks longer then XXO gave Butch when they laid him off.

"Sounds good."

Butch went back to XXO the next day and asked to meet with Joe.

Joe offered, "Have a seat. What's up?"

"I quit." But said with a smile. "What I mean is I found another job and I start a week from next Monday."

"I didn't know you were looking."

"I've been laid off twice in the last two or three months. I've only been called back to catch up on the tapes. Things seem to be slowing down out in the shop."

"That's just temporary. Are you making more money?"

"Just about the same."

"I think we could get you fifty to seventy-five cents an hour raise if you would stay."

"Why am I worth fifty to seventy-five cents an hour more this week than last week?" Butch asked.

Joe didn't know what to say. "Well if you've made up your mind."

"Yes I have. Thanks for hiring me. I enjoyed working here and learned a lot."

CHAPTER THIRTY-SEVEN

*** SHOOT OUT AT OK CORRAL ***

January 19, 1976. What a great day except for the shootout at the OK Corral. Well, a shootout at the Standard Oil Service Station.

Just a few days before Butch was to start his job with MESC, he was looking out the window of Jack's apartment, formerly his parents' apartment, which is located on the second floor of the shop building overlooking downtown Byron.

As Butch was looking out the window he saw some commotion going on down at the Standard Oil Station. The station was only one and a half blocks away and could be clearly seen from the apartment. What happened will be remembered in Byron for a long, long time.

In the morning at about eleven, a car pulled into the station to fill up with gas. In the car were two young people, both in their early twenties.

The man got out of the car and said to the station attendant, Del, "Fill 'er up and check the oil." Remember Butch's childhood friend who almost drank the formaldehyde with Butch in the basement?

209

The woman walked into the gas station lobby. The lobby had a couple of chairs and a desk. On the desk were parts, a phone and the cash register. As the women entered the lobby, she noticed there was no one there.

Del started filling the car with gas and walked to the front of the car and lifted up the hood.

The station owner, Vance, another mechanic named Will, and customer named Hugh were busy out in the garage.

Hugh was the husband to Butch's former high school English teacher. Hugh also used to umpire high school baseball games that Butch played in. He had a big gruff voice and was a tough acting guy, but he was a very nice person.

There was another guy, Ed. Ed owned a business across the street from the Standard Oil Station. He was there just talking with Vance and Hugh.

Everybody knew everybody in this town of six hundred people. The woman looked through a small window between the lobby and the garage. There was also a door between the lobby and garage. The woman saw Hugh, Vance, and Ed in the garage and Del outside. No one else. All was clear.

The women stepped behind the desk, opened the cash register and took less than one hundred dollars.

Meanwhile the man kept Del busy talking while the woman was stealing the money.

From the garage, Vance had noticed the woman when she entered the lobby. He stopped talking with the other men and headed into the lobby. When he entered the lobby, he noticed the woman was taking money from the cash register. Vance shouted to the others in the garage "GET HIM!" pointing to the man talking to Del. "THEIR ROBBING THE PLACE!"

Hugh, Ed and Will came running out of the garage when Vance called for help, and along with Del apprehended the man.

The woman was now in the grasp of Vance, and the men brought the young man into the lobby. Vance, almost threw the young man in a chair, and said to the woman, "Sit there!" pointing to a chair next to the young man. Vance turned to the man, and demanded, "Where's the money?"

"I don't know."

"What do you mean you don't know?" Vance drew back his fist as if to hit the man and said, "Give me the money you stole or I'll knock your head off." Vance didn't know much about Miranda Rights or that you had to treat a thief kindly because he might have had a rough childhood. All Vance knew was the little turd stole his hard earned money.

The young man believed one thing for sure, Vance would smack him. Looking around the room, he didn't see a friendly face in the crowd that was going to help him. The thief reached in his pocket and pulled out the stolen money and gave it to Vance.

"You damned thief! I'm calling the police."

While sitting next to the woman, the man leaned over to her and said "Here take this gun and hide it." The other men in the room were talking about what just happened and what to do, and did not see what was happening.

The woman said," I have to go to the bathroom." Vance said "Okay," and showed her to the bathroom which was out of the lobby in the back of the garage. A couple minutes later, she came out and she and Vance went back to the lobby. As she sat down the man turned to her and said "Go get the gun." The woman looked toward Vance and said, "I have to go to the bathroom again." Vance, "Make this the last time." Vance showed her to the bathroom. A minute or two later she came out of the bathroom, and she and Vance returned to the lobby. As she sat down she opened her purse. The man took the gun and jumped up.

Without thinking, both Hugh and Ed moved toward the pistol wielding thief. In a panic, the young man fired the pistol. Bang! Bang! Two shots. Two bullets hit Ed in the chest. He fell to the floor. Hugh grabbed for the gun and got hold of the man's hand, but the pistol was now pointing straight at Hugh. Bang! Bang! Two more shots fired. Two bullets hit Hugh, one in the stomach, one in the chest. Hugh fell to the floor.

In these same few seconds Del and Will were out the door leading into the garage. After shooting Hugh and Ed, the man saw Del and Will trying to leave the lobby. Del was out the door first. The man fired again hitting Will in the back right shoulder. Will fell down.

Vance, who had been behind the desk near the cash register, had ducked down when all the shooting started.

Del still in the garage and Vance behind the desk, the man and woman ran out of the lobby, jumped into their car and sped off. However, not before Vance had ran after them and got the make and model of the car and part of the license number.

Vance ran back into the garage. Del was now standing in the doorway in half shock looking around. Vance saw Del and asked, "Are you hurt?"

"No."

"How is everyone else?"

"Looks like Hugh, Ed and Will have been shot."

"How are they?"

Will heard and answered, "I'm hit but okay."

Del looked around and finished answering the question. "Hugh and Ed are both hit, looks bad and they're not moving."

Byron hadn't had a real crime in who knows when. Calling the police in Byron is not like calling the police in New York. To get the police in Byron you need to go out to the middle of main street and look up and down the street to see if you can see the police. Remember Byron is a village of six hundred, and there is only one part-time police officer. The policeman is also the village water, sewer, street, and building maintenance person.

The police work is to direct traffic at the Memorial Day parade, attend Friday night football games and chase kids, like Butch in his youth doing mischief about town. If you don't see the police and no one around you knows where he is, you call the emergency phone number.

Who do you get when you call the emergency phone number in Byron? Why, the mortuary, of course. That's right, Lewis N. Small Mortuary. Lewie handles all the emergency calls.

You want the fire department, you get Lewie. You want the ambulance, you get Lewie and his gray Cadillac hearse with white curtains and aluminum sign that reads Lewis N. Small Mortuary on the side window. In a flash the hearse would turn into the Bat Mobile. Well, maybe not the Bat Mobile, but remove the curtains, the sign, and add a red flashing light on top, lay on the siren, and you now have the one and only ambulance in Byron.

The procedure to actually get the ambulance headed to the emergency went something like this: Lewie would get the call, he would call the attendant. Lewie, all three hundred pounds of him, would put the flashing red light on top of the hearse-ambulance, jump behind the wheel and drive to pick up the attendant. This was all done in a matter of minutes depending on where the attendant lived. Lewie's objective as an ambulance driver was getting the patient to the nearest hospital twenty miles away as fast as possible. The attendant would check and treat for bleeding, breathing, and shock. Butch often thought, would Lewie drive a little slower when things were slow at the mortuary? OK, OK, bad thought.

When you wanted the police, it got a little more complicated. If you couldn't see the officer, you called the emergency number and Lewie would call the fire hall to see if the policeman was there. There were no cell phones in 1976. More than likely, there would be no answer. Lewie would then call the *county* police twenty miles away. Most of the time the county had only three or four patrol cars on the road and usually asked Lewie if he would call the *state* police post. The state police had about three or four patrol cars on the road in Shiawassee County and would ask Lewie to call the *county* police. So back and forth from one department to the other it went. No police department wanted to go all the way over to Byron for a police call about someone who stole someone else's watermelon.

Vance told Del, "Call Lewie. Tell Lewie to get down here with the ambulance and have him call Durand for another ambulance." Durand was the closest town to Byron, seven miles away. "Also tell Lewie to hurry up the cops."

Del phoned Lewie. "Lewie, there's been a shooting. Call the police and bring the ambulance. Call Durand for an ambulance and tell the police to hurry."

This time Lewie knew when Del called it wasn't someone stealing watermelons. Lewie didn't know what an understatement it really was. In most cases a call like this to an emergency dispatcher in a large city would be confusing. Not to Lewie. He called Durand for the backup ambulance, then called the county and state police. "This is Lewis Small from Byron. There has been a shooting at the Standard Station in Byron."

Lewie didn't bother to pick anyone up to help him. He knew there would be plenty of people at the scene when he got there. Seconds after the sound of shots, people were heading for the

217

Standard Station. People back then didn't turn away when their fellow man was in trouble. They came running to help even if it cost them their lives.

The county and state dispatched Code Blue, shooting at the Standard Oil Station in Byron. Both state and county police swung into action. Put the pedal to the metal, turn on the light, let the siren blare, push the state police interceptor engine to the max. "We're on our way."

Lewie was at the scene two minutes after hanging up the phone with the police dispatchers. He entered the office of the Standard Oil Station. Vance pointed to Hugh and Ed lying on the floor. Lewie knelt down by Ed, checked his pulse, looked at Vance and shook his head. Lewie looked quickly around the room and went to Hugh.

Pointing in the direction of three men standing nearby, Lewie said, "Put Hugh on the stretcher and put him in the ambulance. Put Ed in the Durand ambulance when it gets here."

Will was now sitting up against a wall half conscious. Lewie said to one of the bystanders, "Give me a hand and we'll send him with Hugh."

Just about then the Durand ambulance arrived with its siren screaming.

Lewie, now outside the Standard Station lobby, about to get into his ambulance, pointed to the lobby to show the guys from Durand where to go. Lewie was off to the hospital with another volunteer at the scene. Durand ambulance attendants entered the lobby and attended to Ed. The Durand team loaded Ed into the ambulance and started for the hospital.

The county and state police arrived just as the Durand ambulance was pulling away. They questioned Vance and Del.

Lewie pulled into the hospital emergency area. Hospital attendants and Lewie wheeled Hugh and Will into the hospital emergency room. A doctor in the emergency room checked Hugh first and said prep him for surgery. Next, Will was seen by the emergency doctor and he said the same thing.

Durand ambulance arrived with Ed. The doctors pronounced Ed D.O.A. The doctor asked Lewie, "Where is the next of kin for Ed?"

"I will have someone call on them," Lewie said. "Best not come from me. No one wants to get a call from a mortician."

219

Ed's family lived three or four miles out of Byron. They had no idea what had happened at the time. Ed was married with three young children, ages between eight and twelve years old.

Hugh had a wife and two adult sons, both married.

Will was hurt but not critically. He would be released in three or four days.

An APB was issued by the State Police, APB all points bulletin issued to all police departments in the state. The young man and woman were arrested getting off a bus in Kalamzoo and delivered to the jail in Shiawassee County where the two were charged with one count of murder and two counts of assault with intent to commit murder.

Hugh was sent home after surgery.

Vance and Del didn't sleep well for the rest of their lives.

Sometime after the shootings, trial began for the young man and woman. The trial took place in Corunna, Michigan, at the county court house. Just as the trial got underway, Hugh was admitted back to the hospital with complications from his gunshot wounds. Hugh's testimony became critical. With everyone looking for cover, Hugh was technically the only one to see which person actually did the shooting.

220

Vance had ducked down behind the desk and couldn't see the shooting. Del and Will had their backs to the shooter as they left the lobby to go into the garage. Ed was lying dead on the floor.

A deposition was taken from Hugh while he was in the hospital. Hugh gave his testimony that the young man was the shooter. The man and woman were found guilty of murder while committing a felony. Both were given life without parole, the man for doing the shooting and the woman for being an accomplice.

Hugh died within a few days after giving his testimony.

Will lives with memories of that day, but leads a normal life.

Del died of alcoholism at the age of sixty-eight.

Vance lived to his mid-seventies with his memories.

Twenty-six years after the conviction, the young woman received a governor's pardon. The woman came from a family that took the time and spent the money to lobby the governor's office for a pardon.

The man's family didn't. He is still in prison to this day.

Shows you what a little money can do. Remember she was the one that had the pistol to start with and she gave the pistol to the man.

Hugh and Ed would not have been shot if it were not for her.

CHAPTER THIRTY-EIGHT

*** FIRST DAY AT MESC ***

"You're going to be working in ES, Employment Services, as an ES interviewer." Ned explained, "You will be interviewing unemployed workers and employed workers that are looking for a different job. I hired you because you had previous sales experience. In the past, MESC was known as the Michigan Unemployment Office. We were moving in a new direction of helping the unemployed find employment. Of course, unemployment insurance will always be a strong part of MESC. We are going to be more employer conscious. The money to run the MESC comes from employers. It is a forced tax on employers' payrolls. Employees do not pay into unemployment compensation."

"I thought part of my pay went into unemployment," Butch said.

"No, you might be thinking of FICA, Social Security, not unemployment. The unemployment tax that an employer pays is used for both unemployment insurance and job placement. We are looking for a person who can go to employers and convince them to list their job openings with MESC. You will go to two weeks of ES training. Then I am sending you one day a week for eight weeks to a new sales training. I want you to be our employer contact guy. You will be going to businesses all over Shiawassee County, plus you will still be a regular ES interviewer. What do you think?"

"Sounds interesting," Butch said, but he thought, "You got to be kidding. It's perfect!" It's all the jobs he's had, selling to supermarkets, real estate, life insurance, underwriter of causality insurance, working in manufacturing, both in the plant as well as the office. Butch couldn't have created a better job. With the biggest smile he said, "I think I'll do just fine."

"Come on," Ned said and they walked a few feet. "This is your desk."

Butch smiled again. This is the desk he was interviewed at two weeks ago. Butch replaced the interviewer who interviewed him. He sat down.

Ned tossed a big thick black book on his desk. "This is the UI-ES manual. It won't make a lot of sense to you right now. It's old, out of

224

date, but that's all we got right now until I can get you scheduled for training. Read as much as you can. The ES interviewers help job seekers obtain work. The UI workers determine eligibility for unemployment compensation. If you have any questions I'll answer them the best I can. I'll be back at noon. I'll take you to lunch. I try to take all new UI-ES interviewers to lunch once on me. After that you're on your own."

Butch looked around. He had been in the office a few times collecting his unemployment. The office was a one story brick building, with one room making up the majority of space with a very open design. There was a lobby where people, known as the applicants, stood waiting to get their unemployment. There was a long counter the full width of the room. On the other side were those god-awful state workers. That's how most of the people drawing their unemployment felt. Butch remembered when he was drawing unemployment a guy in front of him said, "Stand around here two, three hours to get this little unemployment check. That's all those workers have to do. Then they sneak out for a smoke." Butch had said, "Tell you what, I'll stand here for you if you just give me half your check."

"It's lunch time," Ned announced.

Butch wasn't very big but, but he could put the food away. He ate two hamburgers.

"Damn glad I don't have to feed you every day."

At that time there weren't many men employed at the Shiawassee MESC. The three or four men that were employed, weren't particularly close to Ned, so he usually ate alone. Ned took a liking to Butch right off and they started going to lunch every day.

Unemployment was very high nationwide. It was about eleven percent in Michigan, which had been hit hard with layoffs in the auto industry. More and more manufacturing moved to Japan. Michigan's unemployment was approaching thirteen percent. Some of the larger cities where the auto industry was big, unemployment hit over twenty percent. In the areas where Chevrolet, Buick, Fisher Body, AC Spark Plug, and DuPont plants existed, employment fell like a marble falling off a table.

We thought we had it bad in 2009. There were no bail outs, no stimulus package, unemployment, which normally ran for twenty-six weeks, was extended thirteen weeks, then another twenty-six. Nice time to be hired at the MESC. Oh yes, by the way, Butch's job was to find people jobs with an average unemployment rate of twelve to fifteen per cent. Good luck with that.

One of Butch's fellow workers said, "Look at all those people standing in line for unemployment. Isn't it sad?"

Butch answered, "If it wasn't for all those people out there, we wouldn't be here with a job."

As unemployment grew, more and more people were hired at MESC. After a few months there were two more guys hired by Ned. The "good ole boys club" was just starting, and they all went to lunch every day with Ned and Butch. Bob was first, an employment counselor. Bob's job was to help applicants find the right education or training schools. Then Don was hired. Don was a former UI counter worker at the Shiawassee MESC, transferred to ES. Butch, Bob and Don became known as "Ned's boys".

One afternoon coming back from lunch, one of the women said, "Here comes 'Ned's boys'."

Butch turned around with a big smile and said, "You're right."

Ned really didn't show a lot of favoritism to Butch and the

boys. Sometimes men just like to be around men, like women like to be around women.

Butch and the boys were very good at what they did, winning several ES awards. Ned's pat on the back was well earned by the boys.

Gumbo's was the main eating place for the boys but once in a while they would go to the stockyard. The stockyard wasn't the name of a restaurant, it *was* a stockyard. Once a week the farmers would bring in their livestock to be auctioned off to the meat packers in the area. They would bring in cattle, pigs, and sheep. One right after the other, they would be auctioned off. Until noon. Gotta eat! And eat those farmers did! They weren't about to get in their pickup trucks and go to a restaurant. Up above the area where the livestock were housed and auctioned was a large room with several tables set up, a counter and a makeshift kitchen. A restaurant from a nearby town brought in a catered lunch. Man was it good! A lot of it, and very reasonably priced. Plus you got the smell of cows, pigs, and sheep manure on the shoes of the farmers. There was a veterinarian on duty in case something went wrong with one of the livestock. He would come in with a whip about five feet long and snap it and give a whoop and holler. No one knows why he did it but it added some ambiance to the place. He would scare the hell out of you the first time you saw him. The best of all was the aroma. There was still half the livestock to be auctioned. The livestock had been there all day and they weren't bashful about relieving themselves.

A lot of businessmen from nearby towns came to the stockyards for lunch, lawyers from the court house, doctors and other professionals. A joke businessmen would pull, especially on newly hired women was, "Why don't you dress up a little tomorrow and I'll take you to the best lunch in town." They would take them to the stockyard, high heels and all. By the way, it was the best lunch in town!

CHAPTER THIRTY-NINE

*** GOD BLESS ALL VETERANS! ***

Butch's first five years of employment at MESC was as an ES interviewer. The second five years he was the Veterans Employment Representative (VER). Butch interviewed Veterans from World War II, Korea and Vietnam. The vets he interviewed were mainly privates, corporals, sergeants, the ones in the trenches. He not only helped the veterans with employment, he also dealt with special issues some of the vets had, especially the Vietnam veteran. The Vietnam veteran didn't come home to a country that appreciated what they had done. The Vietnam War was very unpopular, with protests and riots. There were no ticker tape parades for the Vietnam vet.

In those days people were labeled as a "dove", a person that was against the war or at least did not think the war should be fought, or a "hawk", one that was in favor of the war.

Butch went from hawk to near dove to hawk again in his feelings about the Vietnam War. Many people said that the Vietnam vets were just potheads. Butch said in the five and a half years he was the

230

veterans employment representative he never heard an unkind word about Vietnam veterans from a veteran that saw action during WWII or Korea. It seemed to him the people that complained the most about those who fought in the Vietnam War were those who never fought at all. One thing Butch could never understand is why we took it out on the vet. They were there risking their lives for the United States, just like the WWII and Korean vets. Many died, lost limbs, lost time. They didn't ask for the war, they just served.

Butch says "shame on us" for thinking less of any vet. We should all be thankful for any person that serves their country, more so for those that actually served under-fire.

The unemployment rate was high among veterans, especially Vietnam vets. Many Vietnam vets would not come into the office for employment help. They just didn't trust government agencies. All veterans received special referral preference on job orders, no matter what era the veteran had served. Veterans were to be sent on job interviews before nonveterans as long as they met the qualifications.

The word needed to get out about job placement for veterans, especially to the Vietnam vets with disabilities. This seemed to be the group that was the most reluctant to seek help. Several federal and state employment programs were created to help them. One was the Disabled Veteran Outreach Worker program known as the DVOW program. The Owosso/Corunna MESC was awarded one DVOW worker.

The first DVOW in the Owosso/Corunna office was Billie. He was a long haired guy with a goatee, happy-go-lucky as could be. Billie was a Vietnam disabled vet with a ten percent rating. He was injured while out on patrol. The tank he was walking beside was hit by mortar fire, leaving him deaf in one ear.

Billie was always in trouble with Ned. Ned would say to Butch, "You gotta do something with him. He's always late, never has his reports in on time." Ned, as Billie would say, "chewed him out". After one of Ned's chewing outs Billie came walking back to the ES area with his legs far apart. When Butch asked him why he was walking that way Billie said, "Ned just chewed my butt out." After another of Ned's chewing outs, Billie came into the area walking normal with a smile on his face. Butch asked what happened. Billie said, "He took his teeth out."

After a few months with MESC, Billie was called for a review of his disability. Reviews were not uncommon. The reviews were conducted at local Veterans Hospitals. Billie's review came back reduced from ten percent to zero, which meant Billie would still have some benefits but would lose the money part of his disability pay. This made Billie, let's say, a little more than pissed off. Billie wrote a letter, no e-mails then, to the Veterans Administration hospital. In the letter Billie suggested that someone should blow up the VA. This, of course, didn't sit well with the VA. The VA called Billie back in for further review. This time they had Billie go to a VA hospital, not for just a physical exam, but a psychological exam as well.

The VA found that Billie wasn't a threat to them or anyone else. They did, however, feel that Billie was under a great deal of stress from his job at the MESC and suggested that he might want to pursue other employment. Billie took their advice and wrote a letter of resignation to Ned. Ned was not a big fan of Billie's, but he knew one thing for sure. Billie would never get a job as good as the one he had at MESC. Ned wrote Billie asking him not to resign. Ned also wrote a letter to the VA asking them to reconsider their advice to Billie. The VA did not change their opinion and Billie resigned.

Billie still lives in the Shiawassee County area. Ned was right. Billie never got another job as good as he had at MESC. As a matter of fact, he never got any other job.

Billie did get married but does not have any children. Billie's income is Social Security. Oh, and by the way, Billie did get his ten percent veterans disability back after another review.

The second DVOW at MESC was Randy. His injury came when he was working in a mailroom on an army base. Randy reached to pick a bag of mail off a conveyor and another large bag hit him on the arm and broke it, hence a disability.

Randy was married with two daughters. He was a motorcycle rider. His favorite saying was, "I'm Randy Buck. I can ride anything with a gas cap."

Randy left employment at the MESC for a job with a company that made powdered milk. After a time, Randy applied for a loan from a local bank to buy a house. The loan was approved based on Randy's job at the powdered milk company. The powdered milk people said what a wonderful worker Randy was. Less than a year later they fired him.

234

Randy went behind on his payments to the bank. He hired a lawyer and sued the milk company. He won. They had to pay off his mortgage. Isn't life sweet? Of course a good lawyer helps.

Randy is doing well and about to retire from the U.S. Postal Service. Go figure!

Butch had his own weekly five minute radio program about veterans' employment on the only radio station in the county. Butch would promote employment service for veterans and service for employers. Butch said there might have been as many as ten or twelve people listening, maybe a few more. A friend of his, a farmer, while plowing in the field heard Butch on the radio. When he went in for lunch, he said to his wife, "Guess who I heard on the radio? Of all people Butch!"

You don't need to bring on the eight by ten glossies just yet. A few years later Butch made some ES training films. Now you can bring on the glossies. He also spoke to service clubs in the area, such as the Lion Clubs and Chamber of Commerce.

Of course, Butch didn't get paid for any of the work he did in the evenings. Butch had worked in private employment and in a family business. He says the people he worked with at MESC were better trained, better educated, more dedicated employees than in any other field he ever worked, and worked for less pay than they would have made outside of state employment. Don't let anyone tell you different. That's why now when Butch hears about "those state employees" he gets a little, let's say, pissed off.

CHAPTER FORTY

*** BEST OF TIMES, WORST OF TIMES ***

Bad times at MESC. No jobs to send laid off workers to. No money for training. The Owosso/Corunna office was one of the most productive offices in the state and Butch had won several awards for job placement and service to veterans. We all know that job performance counts, right? Not so fast. Butch was bumped out of his job at the Owosso/Corunna office.

It's off to the Flint office of the MESC. Flint was not Butch's choice to transfer to. According to union contract, one could only bump or replace someone with lesser seniority within a certain geographic area. Flint was it for Butch.

The manager of the Flint office was Tim Dumasskavich. Butch said Timmy, as he was called behind his back, treated everybody the same, rotten. Timmy was short, thin, white haired, dressed like an undertaker and was as mean as hell.

Every morning employees were to sign in at eight o'clock, not eight oh one. Timmy would stand at the sign in desk with his red pencil and phone in hand, calling time for information. At exactly eight

oh one he would draw what became known as "the line". He would

draw a red line across the bottom of the sign in sheet. If you signed in

late you got chewed out and got docked pay. Timmy never gave extra

pay for working over a few minutes, working through a break or a lunch

and it happened a lot. If you were interviewing someone you couldn't

say "Oh, it's my lunch time." or "It's time for me to go home." You

finished the interview.

Timmy's girlfriend worked in the Flint office. He treated her

the same as anyone else. Of course Timmy's wife never complained. It

would have been difficult from her bed in the nursing home.

It was okay for Timmy to leave early every day to see his wife.

Timmy must have missed her a great deal around four. Didn't miss her

much during most of the day or at night though.

Butch had heard about Timmy, and the poor morale in the Flint

office. First day, first time Butch met the new boss, there he was,

Timmy in the flesh. Butch walked over to Timmy with his hand out

ready for a welcome handshake, and said, "Hi asshole." NO, NO, NO,

not really!

Butch said, "I'm Butch," and before he could say another word, Timmy, without a smile and without shaking Butch's hand said, "Mr. Stiltz is your supervisor," and walked away. Butch, standing there with his hand still out, thought if he had a piece of toilet paper, he could make good use of it.

At the same time, Butch looked up and saw this tall, nearly six foot, slim, dark brown haired, green eye, medium complexion, African-American woman walking toward him, moving everything she had, and she had plenty in a perfect fashion. She put out her hand and said, "I see you met the asshole." And she did say that! "My name is Ann Diller." Ann had several grown children, including twin boys who were both seven feet tall and had trouble written on all seven feet of them.

Ann was a very bright person with a lot of street smarts. Her boys and her husband were in and out of trouble with the law all the time, always relying on Ann to help them out. She was not liked by most of her co-workers, nor did she like most of them. For some reason she and Butch hit it off and became friends.

Butch shook Ann's hand and said, "I'm-"

Ann interrupted and said, "I know who you are. Welcome to

Devil's Island." Ann started walking away and said, "Come with me and I will introduce you to your new supervisor. His name is Duane Stiltz." She added, "You think Timmy was something, wait till you meet Duane."

Butch thought how could he be worse than Timmy? As he approached the supervisor, Ann began, "Duane, this is-"

Now Duane interrupted, "Yes, I know, I've heard about him. I'll show him to his booth."

Duane was a big guy six feet in his mid thirties and just starting to go bald. He was a weightlifter and worked out every day. He had muscles on his muscles. When he looked at you he sort of cocked his head to one side. Come to find out, Duane was blind in one eye.

Duane blamed everything on Timmy. We have to do this or that because Timmy says so. It was just a way for Duane not to take responsibility for anything. When Timmy would holler "Duane", Duane would jump. Turns out Duane was the biggest, strongest wimp around.

The next person Butch met was Harvey. Harvey was a heavyset good ole boy from Tennessee. At first Harvey, with his slow southern

240

drawl would give you the idea that he wasn't very bright. In fact, it was just the opposite. Harvey was one of the more informed and intelligent people Butch knew. He had talked with Harvey several times over the phone about MESC business.

Harvey, Butch, and a man named Bob became good MESC buddies over the years. Bob was an employment counselor at the Owosso/Corunna office. Butch said Bob was the intellectual of the three. Butch would tell Bob, "Keep me informed of the rules and I will do the rest."

Harvey asked Butch, "Did you meet Timmy?"

"Yes."

"Did you meet Duane?"

"Yes."

"Keep your nose clean and to the grindstone for the first month or so and everything will work out. You're a better interviewer than any here."

Butch did exactly that. He got to work early, no red line for Butch, didn't overstay on breaks, didn't leave early for lunch and returned early. At the end of the month during the weekly staff meetings, Duane stood at the head of the room and addressed the staff. "Well, the monthly totals are out." During the month, a women named Pat kept the stats for the ES staff. Pat recorded ES activities such as how many interviews, referrals, placements, everything, and Butch meant everything. She marked every action with a red mark. When you looked at her ledger sheet it looked like a bloodied chicken had walked all over Butch's columns. He led the staff in every area. Not everybody was pleased that Butch, the new guy, was showing them up. For the most part all was okay.

Butch always had a way of getting along with people. He would say, "I can get along with the devil for an hour or two." Duane and Timmy were happy with Butch's performance.

After the meeting Harvey came up and said, "Keep up the good work and everything will work out." Butch was beginning to wonder why Harvey kept saying that. Another month went by with the same result. A few days into the new month, Harvey called Butch back to his desk and said, "How would like to work at the skill center?" Working at the skill center would be like dying and going to heaven, out from under Timmy's watchful eye.

242

The skill center Harvey referred to was a technical school. Each high school in the county could send students for schooling in any number of areas to learn technical skills such as machining, auto repair, graphic arts, plumbing and heating, and so on.

Besides teaching the students, one of the other benefits of the center was job placement. The center would help students get summer jobs and graduates get full time employment. Employers really liked the students from the skill center. Most of the students were average or above in their classes. MESC was asked by the skill center if they would help in the placement process, since MESC had more experience in job placement. The center was a gold mine for MESC. Every student that MESC placed through the center, MESC received credit for placement with the state and placements were what ES was all about. This was perfectly legal and above board. Placements at the skill center was like taking candy from a baby.

Every ES worker wanted the job, many having more seniority than Butch and certainly more seniority at the Flint Branch. All said and done, Butch got the job due to his performance over the two to three months he was at MESC Flint, and the fact that Harvey was pulling for him. Harvey was not well liked by Timmy, but he respected Harvey and Harvey had an outstanding relationship with the head placement guy at the skill center. What Harvey said carried a lot of weight with Timmy.

The head person of job placement at the skill center was John Tower. He was also one of the school counselors. Before teaching at the skill center, John taught in the Flint City School system. His area of expertise, outside of chasing women, was English, in which he had a Master's Degree. John was in his mid fifties with slightly graying wavy hair, very good physical shape, and better than average looking.

Harvey and John had become pretty good pals over the past couple of years. Harvey sold John on letting Butch have the job. After John met Butch, he told Harvey, "Butch seems okay, not as good looking as Annette, but okay." John and Butch hit it off right away. Come to find out, John had just purchased a small farm three miles out of Byron. John would pick Butch up right at Butch's doorstep every day.

Job placement of the students was easy. An employer would call seeking a secretary. Butch would contact the teacher of clerical skills, Reta. Butch would say he needed a person that could type fifty-five words per minute and was excellent in spelling and grammar. The clerical department would have fifty students meeting or exceeding Butch's employer's requirements.

Butch was the leading placement interviewer at the Flint MESC office. ES interviewers were required to place one hundred eighty-five applicants per year to earn their position. As more and more employers left Flint, the placements became more and more difficult. Near the end of the month Duane would ask, "How many you got for me?" meaning how many placements. The Flint staff was always running short on placements. Butch always had placements stockpiled, placements he made but did not turn in everyday or every week. When Duane would call, Butch would say, "Let me look." He would pause and say, "How many do you need, Duane?"

"We're about twenty short."

"I have twenty one, two, three... twenty-four. Yeah, I have twenty four."

"I'll send somebody over."

"Never mind I'll bring them over," Butch offered, and he would deliver the twenty-four placements and still have eight or ten in his drawer for safe keeping. This always helped Butch with placements and helped the Flint MESC as well. As long as Butch worked at the skill center at MESC the Flint office met their placement goals.

Butch enjoyed working at the skill center and having Harvey looking out for him back at the MESC office and John Tower at the skill center. But Butch really wanted to return to the Owosso/Corunna office. As luck would have it, the person that bumped Butch out of the Owosso office wanted to return to Flint. Her name was Maggie Diaz, a Hispanic woman in her late forties.

The bumping process got real crazy. After some mirror flashing and smoke blowing, Maggie returned to Flint, Butch returned to Owosso/Cournna.

Life is good, right? Not so fast. The auto industry slowed down with even more jobs going overseas, factories closing their doors, machinery being moved out, never to be used again. Unemployment was high. Unemployment tax to employers was high. Employers were leaving Michigan, and not many moving in. The politicians wanted to look and sound good so they created programs that train people for the short term. The politicians would say, "Look, we trained three thousand small engine mechanics last quarter." Of course there were only three hundred small engine mechanic jobs. Butch would say, "We have more small engine mechanics than we have small engines."

Life is not so good. Butch is out of work once again. Laid off without any bumping rights. Owosso/Corunna office led the state in job placements, also led the state in job placement for veterans, but was closed. A State Representative from the area in which Owosso/Corunna office was located tried to keep the office open to no avail.

The last day in the office, Butch and his friend, Bob, were waiting for State Office to rescind the closing. The word came down. Bob could and did bump into the Jackson office. Butch got strike three. Butch was laid off without bumping privilege.

CHAPTER FORTY-ONE

*** THE HARNESS BUSINESS ***

Butch did get a phone call about a week before the Owosso/Corunna office closed. The call came from Richard Ruopp of Electrod Wire. Electrod Wire was a private company in Owosso that manufactured wire harnesses. No, not for a horse, for automobiles. Electrod Wire provided wiring for head lights, tail lights, stop lights, etc. There are hundreds of feet of wiring running throughout an automobile. Same with trucks, buses, and airplanes. Electrod Wire made wire harnesses for Ford Motor Co. Electrod Wire employed two hundred ninety to three hundred employees. Almost all the employees were pre-screened and tested for finger hand, eye hand coordination, as well as for color blindness. If you work around electrical wiring, you better not be color blind. All the wiring was color coded, blue stripes, red stripes, orange dots, you name it.

About ninety percent of the employees were women and most of them were Aid to Dependent Children (ADC) recipients, otherwise known as welfare moms. The ADC recipients received money for rent, heat, electrical, food stamps, and medical. The cost of an ADC household could easily be in the thousands of dollars a year. Employing two hundred ninety ADC recipients saved the tax payers a bundle.

Butch had a very nice relationship with Richard Ruopp of Electrod Wire and a sister company called Electrical Mechanical Device. EMD was a manufacturer of electrical components for the auto industry. Everyone who was hired at either EW (Electrod Wire) or EMD (Electrical Mechanical Device) passed through the Owosso/Corunna MESC office. Most of the women had difficult lives. Butch said they looked like they were rode hard and put away wet. One day during a phone call with Butch, Richard Ruopp jokingly said to Butch, "I know you can't pre-screen the referrals based on looks, but could you send me a few that at least have their front teeth?" That was not as much of an exaggeration as you might think.

After receiving the news about layoffs at MESC, Richard Ruopp at EW called Butch.

"You know we have over doubled our employment at EW," Richard told Butch. "Jim and I feel we are in need of a human resource person." Jim Lemmon was the plant manager and general manager for

249

both EW and EMD. "We have been so busy, we've just let things go. The Owosso Fire Chief has been on us about posting fire drills and safety stuff about the weather. Now the feds are after us about hazardous material. We're going crazy. Can you come over and have a talk about being our first human resource person?"

"Sure." Butch was flattered about the call, plus he was unemployed.

"Can you come over tomorrow?"

Butch asked, "What time?"

"How about ten?"

Next morning at 9:45 Butch was at the office.

Richard greeted Butch, "Come on in and have a seat. You know Jim Lemmon, don't you?"

"Sure," Butch said, and everyone shook hands.

"We need a person like you, Butch. You know about our operation here and at Jim's place. We can't quite pay what you were getting at MESC, not at first anyway."

Butch was thinking, "I'm not getting anything from the state right now except unemployment."

250

Richard went on, "I know you come from a manufacturing background, but the wire harness business is different, not as technical as you may be used to, but different. Before going right into the human resource area, we would like you to spend some time in the cutting department."

After a tour of the place and agreement on salary, Butch said yes to the offer and started work the following Monday in the cutting department. This is the department where all the wire is cut to length to go into the harness. The machine that cut the wire ran very fast, cutting lengths of wire from a few inches to several feet long.

Everyone in the cutting department was sent over by Butch from the MESC office. They all knew him. Even the two set up guys. The machine operators, were all women. Remember the ones without front teeth? They had to be super fast to pick up the wire as it came off the machine.

Butch was on his feet more than eight hours a day running from one machine to the other and back again to get more production slips and to read the charts. There was no way he was going to keep up without the help of those toothless women. Butch remembers, without

251

their mercy he would not have made it. They would laugh, in a kind way and say, "No, no, that's not it." The set up guys were even better. When Butch would give them an order to be run and they saw it was wrong, they just grinned and did it right. Butch always took breaks and had lunch with the crew he supervised. He thanked them a lot, which unfortunately they never received much of before.

Butch was quick to admit he didn't know the harness business. Everybody in the plant knew he was just learning the ins and outs, that he was going to be the human resource guy. Maybe that helped.

After a few weeks in the cutting department, Richard called Butch in. "Have you had enough of the cutting department?"

Butch replied, "I thought you were trying to kill me."

Richard laughed and said, "Starting tomorrow you're human resources. The first two things you need to do is call the Owosso fire chief and get him off our backs, then take a look at this hazardous thing. They're really getting on us about this."

"No problem. I would like to meet the workers in the manufacturing area," Butch said.

"All of them?"

"Yes, on a one to one basis."

"You want to call them in here and talk to them, take them off their jobs?" Richard asked.

"No, I want to go out in the plant at their work site and meet them."

"You know we have three shifts here. How are you going to do that?"

"Guess I've got to come in on all three shifts," Butch said.

"Okay with me. But don't forget about the fire chief and that hazardous thing."

During the next three weeks Butch would come in at noon and work half of the first shift and stay on for half the second shift. The next day he would come in halfway through the third shift and stay on until half of the first shift. In this way he could go in the plant four hours a day and meet with the factory workers and still spend four hours a day doing office work, like meet with the fire chief and other office tasks. After a time Butch met all the workers, including janitors, machine operators, material handlers, set up people, everyone. The workers couldn't believe a suit would be out walking around the plant talking to them. A suit was anyone out of the office whether they wore a suit or just a white shirt and tie. Butch was the shirt and tie person.

There always seemed to be a big gap between office personnel and factory workers. Butch knew this from experience doing both. Butch would go over to a work station and say, "Hi, I'm the human resource guy." Most of the workers were very suspicious at first. They would say things like "What do you want?" or "What did I do wrong?" or sometimes nothing. After a while they would loosen up. One of the first people Butch talked with, he asked, "What could be done to make your job easier?" The woman said, "Change everything around."

Butch asked, "What do you mean?"

She repeated, "Change everything around. All the material is on the right side, I'm left handed."

"Did you ever tell your supervisor you were left handed?"

She answered, "No, he always seemed too busy."

Butch had it changed immediately. The woman was so happy she said she would do anything for Butch, and she meant ANY thing. Electrod Wire would be getting more production from the woman. The word got out and the workers loosened up even more.

*** FIRE! ***

"Hello, this is the human resource person from Electrod Wire here in Owosso."

Owosso fire chief barked, "It's about time we heard from you guys. Who did you say this was?"

"Human Resource at Electrod Wire," Butch repeated. "When could you come in and help us?"

A few days later the fire chief and his two assistants arrived.

Butch greeted the fire chief. "Hello, chief, glad you all could make it. Let's start in the manufacturing area first, if that's alright with you." Out the door, turn right.

Fire chief started right in, "See there that fire extinguisher? It's the wrong one, too small. Looks like it hasn't been inspected since the day you put it up."

"All that is going to change today," Butch promised. After the inspection he said, "I will call you when we have corrected everything. Butch had a list pages long.

When Butch saw Richard he said, "Here, Richard, is the list of items we need to make the fire chief happy."

Richard looked quickly over the items. "Get everything he wants and see that it is placed exactly where he wants it. All fire extinguishers, right size, right kind, right place."

Second visit by the fire chief.

Again Butch greeted him, "Hi, chief, let's get started. Let me know if there is anything you want changed."

After a complete inspection, the chief said, "Perfect, just the way we wanted it."

"Chief would you stop in and say hello to Richard Ruopp, our plant manager?" Butch asked.

"Oh yes, I've met him before," the chief agreed.

"Richard," Butch said, "the chief would like to give you an overview of the inspection he has just completed."

"Of course I will send you a more formal report but an informal report would be good job!"

When the informal report was over Butch turned to the chief and said, "Come back anytime, send me any updates on fire safety that you might think we can use."

The fire chief left.

Richard then told Butch, "Now if we can just get that hazardous thing done."

*** HAZARD ***

Hazardous Communication Act was a federal law that required employers to inform their employees of any hazardous materials they might come in contact with while doing their job. About the time Butch started working for EW, the law was in full swing. All employers big and small, and all types of employment had to have a hazardous communication program.

Butch didn't know much about the law, but he did know a lot of employers. One of the employers in the area that worked with hazardous material was a battery manufacturer. The battery company made automobile batteries for the auto industry. Batteries contain acid and lead. The contents of the battery, if exposed, could cause cancer. Women of child bearing age could become sterile. Butch knew the human resource person at the battery company. Butch had worked with him during his days at MESC.

Butch placed a call to Pete Moure at the battery company and Pete invited him to look over his hazardous communication program. Butch knew if the battery company's program met the federal specifications they would work for EW. Butch met with Pete.

"Here is a booklet and a video that lays out the company's and employees' responsibilities." Pete said. "At the end of each section there is a sign off section where the employee signs and dates that they received the instruction."

Butch said, "Wow, that must cost a pretty penny."

"Why don't you take the tape and copy it off? Offered Pete. "I didn't see anywhere that you couldn't copy it, same with the booklets. Copying them would be cheaper than buying them. Come on out in the plant and I'll show you how we do our posting."

After the tour Butch said, "How can I pay you back?

"You were always fair with me on referrals, you did our testing and pre-screening. If I can help a fellow H.R. person, I will."

"Maybe we can do lunch," Butch said

"That would be great."

Butch said, "I'll take you to the stockyards."

Back at EW, Butch laid out his program to Richard who was thrilled.

"This needs to be done during work time when everyone is here. We will have to do it in small groups," Butch told him. "We'll do third shift the last hour and a half, first shift when they first come on, and then stay over an hour and a half and do second shift."

Butch set up the sessions. Richard attended part of two sessions. Remember the group we are about to train: former hardcore, down on their luck, welfare moms. Some drank too much, some did a little drugs. All had been around the corner, so to speak. During one session, Butch said that there could be cancer causing agents in some of the material they were handling and some of the material could cause women to become sterile. One woman raised her hand and said, "I can't get knocked up anymore anyway, but you can try if you want." Butch did say he didn't think he could be made to blush, but the ladies

259

at EW did. There was a lot of joking by the women, some made notes or critiques that were handed in at the end of the training. Richard was a little upset about it.

Butch said, "It's the first time they felt that comfortable about speaking out."

After the training sessions for hazardous communication at the Owosso plant was over, Richard called Butch into his office. "You did a real nice job on the hazardous program. I mentioned it to Mr. Stelzer at the corporate office in Southfield." Mr. Stelzer was not only president of Electrod Development in Owosso but also plants in Texas and Indiana. He and his son owned one hundred percent of the corporation. Mr. Stelzer was in his mid to late sixties, tall, a very distinguished looking man. His son looked about the same, only in his early forties. To say the least, Mr. Stelzer and his son carried a very big stick in the corporation.

*** TRAINING DAY ***

Richard announced, "Everyone is here, two or three from each plant, plant managers, human resource people, including Mr. Stelzer and his son." The training had gone well. At one point during a training, Mr. Stelzer gave a wrong answer and Butch, before thinking, corrected him. Mr. Stelzer got a big laugh out of it.

A week later Richard called Butch into his office. "Mr. Stelzer got a bang out of your presentation. He liked it so much he wants you to go to the plants and give the presentations yourself."

"I thought he wanted someone from each plant to do their own?" "No," he told Butch, "everybody agreed, you should do it."

That would mean Butch now had to train all the other employees in all the other states.

In the meantime Butch got a recall letter from the State of Michigan for an opening at Social Services in Corunna, the very same office that his wife Diana worked. When an employee of the state receives a permanent lay off, they are put on a recall list for any jobs that they are qualified. Butch liked working at Electrod Wire, but had over ten years of seniority toward retirement with the state. He had also been hearing a lot of talk about Electrod Wire and her sister companies moving to Mexico.

When Butch got the notice of recall he confronted Richard and asked if the rumors were true. Richard told him yes, they would be moving in the next six months to a year to Juarez, Mexico. Butch didn't understand all that goes into making a move like this.

Butch asked, "Do you think they will be able to manufacture wire harnesses as well in Mexico as in the United States?"

"Sure, why not? We will move all the machinery, production lines, fixtures, everything to Mexico. All the engineering and office personnel will move, too."

"To Juarez, Mexico?"

"No, to San Antonio, Texas, just a few miles from Juarez. Live in San Antonio, work in Juarez. The labor cost is much lower."

At that time Electrod Wire was paying five dollars and eighty-five cents an hour, which was a decent wage for Owosso, plus hospitalization. In Juarez, Mexico the wage was six dollars day, no hospitalization, no social security tax on employers, no unemployment tax, no worker compensation tax. Same quality and production as in the United States. No brainer, move to Juarez.

So what do we do with the two hundred ninety employees who work at EW, those women that came from welfare? They go back on welfare. At that time the politicians said the low end jobs like those at

EW were not the type of jobs that would be missed. They said they would train them in other areas.

The politicians were letting the very jobs unskilled laborers could do slip away to Mexico. Remember what Ross Perot said, "Can you hear that sucking sound? That is American jobs going to Mexico." The politicians said we will retrain the displaced worker and they did. Now we will train all the ladies laid off from industry to become beauticians! The only thing we have more of in Shiawassee County than small engine mechanics is beauticians . What did we get from Mexico?

CHAPTER FORTY-TWO

*** TO BE OR NOT TO BE A SOCIAL WORKER ***

Changing jobs again. Butch accepted the recall and started working for Social Services. He would be a case worker interviewing applicants to determine eligibility for Aid to Dependent Children, Food Stamps, Medical Assistance and Emergency Assistance. Some applicants come into Social Services without a place to sleep or without food. Most had minor children and decisions had to be made on the spot.

The rules and regulations all came down from Mount High. Law- makers made changes; they listened to groups from the so-called left and right. Staff meetings were held every week at social services. The main topic was change. Butch said he never saw so many changes. Sometimes the changes were changes to the changes. One example was "Will the women who are pregnant be able to get Aid to Dependent Children for the unborn child? At first the answer was no. The child was not yet born, so was not eligible. Then yes, the mother had certain needs and, after all, their was a child but not yet born. Butch just

264

couldn't keep up. Too many rules, too many changes. He did not receive any formal training. He was given manuals that were already obsolete. Outside of that, it's a pretty good manual.

On Butch's first day, Dan, the Director of the Owosso office, called Butch in. Butch had met and knew Dan from his days at MESC. Dan, Ned, and the MESC branch manager were very good friends. On occasion Ned and his boys, of which Butch was one, would go to lunch with Dan and his boy, Matt. It happens that the Shiawassee County Department of Social Services and the Owosso/Corunna MESC was in the same pole barn office building.

Dan said he was glad to have Butch on board and that Mary Ann would be his staff manager. Mary Ann was a little wisp of a women, one hundred ten pounds at most, about five feet two. Her hair was jet black, very straight and long, with dark brown eyes. Workers under her supervision either liked her or didn't, no in between. Butch's wife, Diana, had worked with Mary Ann before she became supervisor. She had also been Diana's supervisor and they had hit if off well. Butch had also met Mary Ann over the years and felt comfortable with the idea of her being his supervisor.

Dan walked Butch over to Mary Ann's office. She shook Butch's hand and said, "Have a seat." With a slight smile on her face she said, "This isn't going to be like MESC." The hair on the back of Butch's neck started to stand up a little. Mary Ann's smile returned, and everything was alright again, or was it?

Butch asked, "You do know that Diana and I have a trip planned to visit my brother in California for two weeks? Is that going to interfere with my training or anything?"

Mary Ann answered, "Oh no."

Liar, liar, pants on fire! That will come later.

Back from sunny California where Michigan blew a thirteen point lead and lost to Arizona State in the Rose Bowl, but that's another story. First day back Butch entered Mary Ann's office. She said, "Welcome back. Have a seat." She tapped her finger on two large stacks of files. "This is your case load. All one hundred fifty-five. If you need any help, let me know or someone on your staff can help with an occasional question."

"You mean I have a full case load with no more training than I've had?"

266

Mary Ann answered, "Well, you missed two weeks. The cases can't wait."

"I thought you said it wouldn't interfere with my training?"

"The other caseworkers had to work your caseload while you were training and on vacation," she said. "They will help you and so will I." Mary Ann's pants are really on fire now!

Butch tried as much as he could but he just wasn't getting it. Workers with years of experience were taking stress leave. Everyone was complaining about the changes and the work load. Several workers worked through breaks, lunch hour, even stayed after work to get caught up. The other workers on Butch's staff did help all they could. One woman, Beth, did more than the others. Diana helped too. Diana had her own caseload and was on another staff, but she helped every day, every break. Butch and Diana worked through their lunch hour, eating while working. They stayed late almost every night for an hour or so and came in every Saturday for three or four hours. No one received pay for the extra hours worked. Management eventually said that no one could stay after work or come in on Saturday without a supervisor being present. Butch started talking to others that had Mary

267

Ann for a trainer. One of the caseworkers, Carol, told Butch she and others had a very difficult time with Mary Ann's training. Butch had worked with Carol at MESC. She was an adjudication worker at MESC in Owosso. Adjudication work was similar to Social Service work. In both jobs you had to apply rules and regulations to determine eligibility. Carol was a little different in her appearance. She was more like one of the leftover flower children of the 1960s, but she was well educated and one of the better workers. If Carol had a difficult time learning from Mary Ann, Butch knew he didn't stand a chance.

Butch had just received his three month performance report from Mary Ann. This was standard for new employees. It wasn't good. Unsatisfactory. Push had come to shove. Butch made an appointment with Dan Lazer.

Butch felt good talking to Dan Lazer because of their previous relationship. He knew he could be open and straight forward. Butch told Dan, "I just can't get it. I've had a lot of different jobs in my life, but I just can't get this."

Dan laughed, "It's different from what you were used to at MESC." "I know it's different, it's not the difficulty, it's Mary

Ann. She's got to be the worst trainer I've ever known. I didn't get the formal training the others received. Mary Ann's one on one training is awful. I asked others that had her as a trainer and they say the same as I do. Dave, would you move me to another staff, or fire me?"

"I am not going to fire you. If things don't work out with Mary Ann, I will move you to another staff."

Butch had already talked to another staff supervisor, Polly, about his trouble with Mary Ann. She, said if it was alright with Dan and Mary Ann, she would take Butch on her staff.

Dan said maybe it would be a good idea if he, Mary Ann and Butch had a meeting and aired everything out. Butch said, "Great."

At the meeting, Dan opened discussion. "Who wants to start?"

Complete silence. Not a word. Then Butch said, "I'll start." He let his hair down, let it all out.

Dave, "Mary Ann, do you have anything to say?" Not a word. She just sat there, looking straight ahead. Then Dave asked her, "Mary Ann, would you rather talk in private?" Mary Ann nodded her little blank head. Dave looked at Butch and said, "Well, I guess that will be all for now." Mary Ann didn't have the guts to say anything about

Butch to his face in front of Dan Lazer. After the meeting with Mary Ann, Dan called Butch back in. Butch was made as hell. Dave said, "Don't worry, you are not going to be fired as long as I am director here. We will transfer you to Polly's staff on Monday. Until then just relax."

Relaxing was something that Butch was not good at, but he thought everything would work out and work out it did. But not at Social Services. Butch knew it was not going to work. He hated the job at Social Services. One change after the other, not really helping anyone, just reading the manual, making the changes. If the client meets the requirements and jumps through the hoops, they received welfare.

CHAPTER FORTY-THREE

*** BACK TO MESC AGAIN! ***

Butch remembered that he was still on the recall list for MESC. Being hired by the Department of Social Services did not remove his name for recall with MESC.

Recalls worked something like this. If you had your name on a recall for the Flint MESC only and the Lansing office sent a request to fill an opening, you would not be notified. You had to put your name on a specific office recall. Butch knew he was on the Flint recall list, but didn't know if he was the Lansing list. Both Flint and Lansing would be equal distance for him to drive. He first called a friend he had worked with at both the Owosso and Flint MESC offices, Jennie McGray. Jennie lived just outside Owosso. If there was an opening in Lansing, Jennie would know. Butch made the call to Jennie.

"Jennie, is there going to be any openings that you know of in Lansing?

"As a matter of fact there is going to be four in the next four months."

How great can that be! Butch called MESC State Office. "I am calling to find out if my name is on the recall list for Lansing?"

Dummy, I mean person on the other end of the phone, said, "No."

Butch went on, "Can I put my name on recall for Lansing?"

Pause. "Yes."

"How much time do I have left on recall?"

Pause. "I'm not sure I can give you an answer."

"Who can?"

"My supervisor."

"I would like to speak to your supervisor," Butch said.

"This is Brenda, recall supervisor. What can I do for you?"

I guess the pause person couldn't relay the information. Butch gave his name and said that he would like to have his name put on the recall for the Lansing office and that he would also like to know how much longer he would be eligible for recall.

Brenda told him, "I need more information than your name."

"What information do you need?"

"Your social security number, the office you were laid off

272

from."

Butch gave her his social security number and told her he had been laid off from the Owosso office.

"Do you know the office number?" Brenda asked.

Butch thought, "You got to be kidding! How many offices do you think there were in Owosso?" but he said, "Number eighty-one".

"Just a moment. I see you took a recall to the Department of Social Service in Owosso."

"Yes, I still have recall to MESC offices, don't I?" he asked.

"Yes."

Butch was fighting for his employment life. "Is my name on the recall list for Lansing?"

"No."

"I would like to put my name on the recall for Lansing office."

"You need to notify the State Office by mail."

"You mean I can't do it by phone? I gave you my name, the office and office number that I worked at and social security number."

"Notification has to be in writing."

"Can I send notification to your attention?"

"Yes."

"Will you call me and let me know if you received it and that I am on recall for Lansing?"

"We normally do not do that."

"Can I call you?"

"Yes."

"What is your extension number?"

"Two one one"

Butch sent the request that day by special delivery, return receipt requested. Two days later Butch got a call from Brenda. "We normally do not make contact by phone, but I know how much this means to you. I received your request for recall to Lansing. I would also like you to know we just received a request from the Lansing office to fill an Employment Interviewer position, and you will be receiving a recall from State Office. If you accept, you will be given a date and time to start work."

Butch was elated, "Brenda if you were here I would kiss you."

Brenda laughed, "Well, I don't know about that."

Butch checked the box on the form accepting recall to the

Lansing Office. In a few days Butch received the date and time to

report to the branch manager of the Lansing MESC.

CHAPTER FORTY-FOUR

*** LANSING OFFICE ***

(life is good again)

The branch manager was Melva Dillson, a tall slightly heavy woman. Melva dressed well, carried herself with her head up, had a very professional air about herself. When you took a closer look at her face you saw a different person. One that had seen hard times, a lot of them. Melva was born in Mississippi, in the early 30s, at a time and place it wasn't fun to be an African-American. Melva's father was a tenant farmer.

Melva's parents knew that Mississippi wasn't the place they wanted to raise a family. It wasn't easy to move a family from one state to another when you didn't have any money or a marketable skill for work. Melva's father was lucky. He had relatives in Detroit, Michigan that helped him move and helped him gain employment as a janitor in an office building and her mother as a nurse's aide in a Detroit hospital. Inner-city Detroit in the early 40s may not have been the best place to live in the world but it had Mississippi beat seven ways to Sunday.

Melva was a very intelligent person. She graduated from high school, enrolled in a nursing program, but after one year she had to drop out for lack of money. She needed to contribute to family needs. She worked as a nurse's aide at the same hospital as her mother. As time rolled on, Melva stayed employed, working sometimes full time, sometimes part time.

Melva married a man who worked at Ford Motor Company. For the most part she had good a life. By the early 70s employment got better. She, with the encouragement of friends, took a state civil service test and began working at a Detroit MESC office as a clerk, then E.S. Interviewer to E.S. Supervisor to Manager of the Lansing MESC.

Butch later said he learned a great deal from Melva about the difficulties that minorities face during the 30s, 40s and up. Melva and Butch became good friends during the time Butch worked under her supervision.

The first day Butch signed in and went to Melva's office. Manager and supervisor office spaces at MESC were not enclosed. They were open booth type cubicles with walls only five feet high. There were no doors, just an opening in one of the walls. Managers

277

and supervisors could stand up and look over their entire staff. When Butch reached Melva's office-booth, Melva was standing in the entrance.

Butch said, "Hello, I'm-"

Before he could say anything more, Melva said, "I know who you are. See that man standing over there?" She pointed toward a heavyset man in his late 50s. "That's Cliffton Mack. He is your supervisor. Report to him."

Butch was thinking this is deja vu all over again. The same welcome Timmy D. gave him in Flint. "Thanks, I would like to thank you for hiring me in Lansing."

Melva said, "I had nothing to do with it. You were on the recall list and here you are. Cliff will fill you in on the do and don'ts." She turned and walked to her desk. Butch said to himself, "Yep Timmy D in drag."

Butch strolled off toward the booth of the ES supervisor, Cliff Mack. Cliff was a very well educated man who spoke fluent Spanish and French and taught at the high school level before working at MESC. Butch looked up and there was Cliff looking across the room.

Cliff didn't see Butch walking toward him.

Butch, my God, it looks as though he has his finger in his nose up to the second joint! Cliff turned toward Butch. No. Cliff did not have his finger in his nose. It now looked as though Cliff's right index finger was missing at the second joint. Oh, yes that's it!

Cliff stuck out his right hand, the one with the missing index finger. Butch shook Cliff's hand.

Cliff said, "I am Cliff Mack, ES supervisor. I'll show you to your booth. Jennie has told us all about you."

Butch joked, "I hope she lied and said something nice.

"Oh yes," Cliff laughed. He seemed like a strange duck. Not just the missing finger, just strange.

Butch did what he did in Flint, threw himself into his work. Always early, didn't over extend breaks, got back from lunch on time, did a good job, got along well with fellow workers. He told Jennie that the Lansing office didn't seem like a big office, more like a large Owosso office.

After a few months Butch was the unspoken, and unpaid lead worker. When issues with applicants came up, Cliff would say, "Give

279

them to him," pointing to Butch, then he would make like Elvis and "left the building." Butch became the employer contact person and made most of the PTC, Promotional Telephone Calls, calling employers on the phone about jobs, and so forth.

Butch also made most of the employer visits. On one of Butch's employer trips, he noticed a huge building that had been sitting empty for some time. There were a few cars parked in the parking lot. He drove to the plant, went inside and asked what was going on. The construction workers said a new plant called Hayes was going to be moving in.

Back at the Lansing office Butch called and talked to the person that was going to be the head of human resources. She said that Hayes would be hiring two or three hundred employees, that she was about to start running ads in the local paper. Butch explained that MESC could register applicants, test, and set up interviews for her. She wanted to meet with him. After the meeting, Hayes ran all their applicants through the Lansing MESC. The plant ultimately employed seven hundred fifty employees. The Lansing office of MESC received all the new hires plus all hires in the future.

Needless to say, this put a big feather in Butch's hat. Melva was knocked off her feet. She became close to Butch, bringing him into manager meetings and showing him off like a prize pony. Melva and Butch became so close that Butch was a steady lunch companion of Melva, Dill the assistant manager, and Evelyn the new ES supervisor. Looked a little like Owosso MESC and Ned's boys! Clifton Mack retired and Butch found out what was so strange about Cliff. He liked boys more than girls, a lot more! No place in the school system for Cliff, hence MESC.

The new ES supervisor was Evelyn. Evelyn was a short, stout, very average looking person, unmarried, with two little girls to raise. Evelyn's husband was a drunk and a wife beater. One night he shot himself, so they say. Evelyn found him with three bullets in the head. Not really! But he did kill himself, so they say.

Evelyn originally hired into MESC as an ES interviewer. A few years later she got her first job as a supervisor. Evelyn was an in your face, I'm the boss type of supervisor. She wasn't that well educated, only having a high school diploma, and had no experience in the world of business. Most of her jobs were lower end employment until she started at MESC.

Evelyn came in with a big smile concealing her attitude of I'm boss and you are going to do it my way. After a few staff meetings, Evelyn found her ways of running the ES staff in Lansing weren't working. Butch told her, "Maybe we should look at that in a different way."

Evelyn, I think my way is best."

Butch said, "Okay."

Later, other staff members would confront Butch and say, "You know that's not going to work."

Butch would advise, "Give her enough rope to let her hang herself. She'll come around."

Sure enough, Evelyn would change back to the former way of operation or do what Butch suggested. After a while Evelyn would talk over changes with Butch before staff meetings.

*** THE ITALIAN STALLION ***

The gossip around the staff was they were getting a new transfer. At a staff meeting Evelyn said it was true.

"We don't like to repeat gossip," Butch said, "so listen close the first time." The new transfer was a very special, or let's say notorious interviewer. His name was Gary. Gary was a tall, over six feet, trim one hundred seventy-five pounds, black wavy hair, dark brown eyes, smooth tan complexion. A real Italian stallion. Life at MESC in Lansing was never going to be the same again. Gary had a smile that made women cross their legs every time he came into the room.

Before coming to Lansing, Gary lived and worked in the Detroit area. In the past year or two Gary worked in three different MESC offices, one step ahead of a woman he had pissed off. One of his women tried to shoot him. The only reason she didn't kill him was she wasn't a very good shot. One stabbed him. Gary got away with only superficial wounds. One woman did hit him with a car, causing bumps and bruises. Gary was in good shape and bounced well. After a few close calls, Gary decided that maybe he should get out of Dodge.

Butch saw Gary just after his short interview with Melva. On the way out Butch and Gary just nodded to each other. Melva walked over to the ES section of the office, stood beside Evelyn's booth and made a general announcement that he would start tomorrow and walked away.

Evelyn announced there would be a staff meeting in the morning to meet Gary. Everyone had heard at least a little about Gary. No one really knew what was to come. Next morning at the staff meeting, Evelyn introduced Gary. Butch was right, every women had to cross her legs to stop their insides from falling out. There he stood, straight and tall, white shirt and tie, with the biggest and brightest smile. He said, "Hello."

Butch never met a person that could walk into a room and catch every woman's heart, even if they did know he was the biggest womanizer in the world. Gary was a Don Juan, a Casanova, an Elvis rolled into one. Gary was a stud and he knew it. He could actually enter a room full of women and in ten minutes know which one he was going to take to bed that night. After the staff meeting Evelyn took Gary on a tour of the ES staff. When Gary came to Butch's booth they shook hands. Butch said, "See ya later." Gary just nodded. Butch and Gary both seemed to know "you know I know you know" type of thing without saying a word. Gary was no dummy. He knew the branch manager, Melva. He knew she was from the Detroit area and knew about him. He also knew of the Lansing MESC's good reputation for being one of the state's top performing ES offices. He might also have heard of Butch.

After landing Hayes and Eastern Wheel accounts (Eastern Wheel another company employing over six hundred people) Butch became one of the ES trainers for the state of Michigan, Butch was becoming quite well known.

Later after the staff meeting, Gary came over to Butch's booth.

Butch said, "Have a seat. I hear you are a leather neck." Which was slang for Marine.

"Yeah, you?"

Butch replied, "No, my brother, Jack, was in the Marines during Korea." If you were a Marine or could talk halfway intelligent about the Marines or military, you were Gary's friend. The only thing Gary liked more than women was the Marine Corp or maybe vice versa. At any rate, Butch and Gary hit if off. Gary had one female conquest after another. On Monday mornings Butch would call Gary over to his booth and say, "Gary, tell me about your weekend. I think my heart can take it."

Gary didn't like Evelyn at first, but after a while it grew into a real hatred. He couldn't stand to see Evelyn, hear her, or talk about her. The rest of the staff, for the most part, just didn't respect her. Gary would do only what he had to, like being in the Marines, he never volunteered for anything. When Evelyn would ask him to do something he would just look at her with one of his I-would-like-to-kill-you looks.

*** HE IS GOING TO KILL 'EM ***

Another worker in the office was Barbara. To say the least she was weird. She believed in things like tea leaf reading. Gary scared Barbara to death. He would just look at her with his I-would-like-to-kill-you look, and Gerry would want to run and hide. Gerry would go to Butch and say, "Gary is going to kill me!"

"He's not going to kill you today."

The situation got so bad that Gerry transferred to the Flint office. Gary really didn't hate Gerry, he was just having his kind of sick fun.

All of a sudden Butch heard, "Come quick, he's going to kill em!" "Who is going to kill who?" Butch was at the front counter where there was trouble again. When some applicant got pissed off they would come and get Butch. Butch seemed to be able to calm the irate applicant down. First, Butch would get them away from the front counter where there weren't other applicants to show off in front of. He would escort them to his booth. Now, the applicant would be out of their element and into Butch's. He would have them sit down and he would say, "I will answer all of your concerns. You may not like the answer, but I will give it to you straight." It seemed to work.

"Now who is Gary going to kill today?"

"Three little Vietnamese."

"What?" Just as he and the counter worker approached, she

pointed and said, "See!"

Gary was standing on one side of the counter, face red with anger, eyes bulging, veins sticking out on his forehead and neck, spit flying as he spoke in what Butch thought might be Vietnamese. On the other side of the counter were three very little people standing very close together with a look of terror, believing Gary really was going to kill them.

Butch approached Gary from the front so Gary could see who was coming at him.

"Come on Gary, let's talk it over."

"I should just kill em," Gary raged.

"We're not killing anybody today, Gary," Butch said as he gently touched Gary's right elbow and started walking back to his desk. "Ok, Gary, why are we killing those three poor little Vietnamese people today?"

"Poor little Vietnamese people, my ass! A couple years ago they were paying me to kill em, now they want me to get them a job!"

"Well, they're not paying you to kill em now." Just then Evelyn walked up to Butch's booth.

288

Evelyn addressed Gary, "We need to talk." Evelyn had her Gary-face on. This was going to be Evelyn at her stupidest. Gary looked at her with a look that sent chills up and down Butch's spine. He really will kill her this time, he was sure of it, and Butch thought "I just might let him."

Butch redirected Gary's attention. "Gary, why don't you go to the breakroom, have a coffee and a smoke. When you feel like you don't want to kill Evelyn, come on back." He turned to Evelyn and said, "Evelyn, have a seat." Then asked, "Do you really want Gary to kill you?"

"He had no right to treat those Vietnamese people that way. Something should be done about Gary."

"He could go on sick leave for three or four months. See a shrink. It wouldn't do any good. I'm sure he's done that before. Then he'll come back real happy with you," Butch created the picture for her. "In the meantime we will be without an interviewer. Evelyn, why are we having Vietnam Vets interview Vietnam people?"

"Can't make any exceptions."

Butch asked, "Why not? There can't be that many Vietnamese

people in Lansing. I don't think it is just Larry who doesn't want to interview Vietnamese. Will and Joe aren't that interested either." Will, the office VER, was injured by a landmine, and still had pieces of metal in his back and leg from the Vietnam War. Joe, the office DVOW, was also a Vietnam Vet. "Evelyn, why not have someone else interview the few Vietnamese when they come in? If anyone looks Vietnamese send them to me or someone else. Everybody, including the Vietnamese, will be happy."

Evelyn agreed. "Okay, but I don't like it."

Everything is good again. For a minute.

"Hurry, he's going to kill *her* this time!"

On the way to the front counter Butch asked, "Who's Gary going to kill now?"

Front counter worker, "EVELYN!"

Butch said, "We better hurry, he really might."

Gary, "You're stupid, you're ignorant, you're..."

Butch got him and said, "Come on, Gary, let's talk it over."

Gary

was at his best! Red faced, veins sticking out, spit flying all over everyone within ten feet! "Sit down, Gary. What happened?"

"She's stupid, she's ignorant!"

"Okay, okay. You've already said that."

"She's fat!"

"What?"

"She's fat, she's got more chins than a Chinese phone book!"

"I don't care how many chins she's got, you can't kill her today. Gary I've got some good news for you."

"Is she terminal?" Gary asked.

"No, Evelyn got promoted to Branch Manager."

"Not here?!"

"No."

Gary "That figures." Peters principle at work. "Who's going to replace her?"

"They haven't made that decision yet."

*** EVELYN'S OUT, WHO'S IN? ***

When the staff heard that Evelyn was leaving they all signed a petition to have Butch made staff supervisor. Butch did not know this for a long time. He was on the register for supervisor, but there were two people who were already supervisors and were requesting transfer. Both Jane and Vedo had been on the ES staff in Lansing. Jane was a very likeable person with just over six months as an ES supervisor and Vedo with about the same experience. The person doing the hiring was Kirk. Kirk had just been promoted as Lansing Branch Manager upon the retirement of Melva.

Kirk was a short, five feet three, stout, one hundred eighty pounds, an educated computer type guy. Kirk had the personality of a popcorn fart. He wasn't one to rock the boat. He didn't like to make tough personnel decisions, or any decisions for that matter. If he was to hire Butch over two so called experienced supervisors he would have to write a letter of exception stating why he thought Butch, without supervisor experience, would be better than either of the other two. He could have used the letter the staff gave him as a recommendation. Butch had also been acting supervisor on two different occasions. No, it would be easier just to hire one of the other two. So Kirk hired Jane.

Unlike Kirk, Jane made all kinds of decisions, most of them wrong. Jane knew one thing, make Butch her official lead worker. Jane

292

convinced Kirk to put in for a lead worker for the Lansing ES office. Kirk, feeling a little guilty about not hiring Butch as supervisor, agreed.

Butch became ES lead worker with all the responsibility that went with it. Lead workers were like top sergeants in the Army. They run the day to day operations, and the second lieutenant, if they're smart, let them. As lead worker Butch would make work assignments, take care of problems, you know, kind of what he had been doing the last few years. And the pay? Well, it zoomed up to a dollar an hour more, forty bucks a week. Oh well, a dollar is a dollar.

Life is getting better.

CHAPTER FORTY-FIVE

*** PAPER, PAPER EVERYWHERE ***

Government ran on paper. The way to fix government is throw money and paper at it. Of course that never worked, but the government hadn't figured that out. MESC was no exception. ES was the worst of the worst. Every person who was drawing unemployment had to be registered with Employment Services. People working but wanting to change jobs could be registered with ES, and thousands of people not working or drawing unemployment could be registered with ES looking for work. Large offices such as Lansing, Flint, Detroit, would have upward of twenty-five thousand people actively seeking work.

Each person had to fill out a form known as the twenty-five eleven. The twenty-five eleven contained all the information on an applicant such as name, education, training, work history, address, and so on. The form itself was a normal size piece of paper, as thick as a post card. The form was folded in half and filed in drawers. The drawers were kept in the front counter. Usually the front counter was served by three or four counter workers.

294

When an applicant came into the office their twenty-five eleven was pulled, date stamped, and referred to an ES interviewer. People receiving unemployment and anyone wanting to remain active to be referred for employment had to come into the office and have their twenty-five eleven stamped once a month. If they didn't, their twenty-five eleven was purged from the active file and put into an inactive file.

The normal procedure for registering an applicant was to have them fill out a paper twenty-five eleven, sit down with an ES interviewer and the ES interviewer would then enter all the information from the twenty-five eleven into the computer. At each subsequent interview, the interviewer would annotate on the form what happened during the interview and also make the same entry into the computer.

The last working day of the month was purge day. All ES staff helped purge the files. Talk about your labor intensive, high paper volume! How would you like to be the guy who supplied the twenty-five eleven forms to MESC? That same guy probably supplied the hundreds of thousands twenty-three sixteens, which was a job order form. Each job placed by an employer had to have a twenty-three sixteen. Each twenty-three sixteen had two parts, each eight and a half by sixteen, with a carbon paper between. A lot of paper, a lot of cost. The so called brain thrust in the main office of the State MESC recognized the problem was too much paper so they, whoever they were at State Office, named a committee to solve the problem.

*** THE COMMITTEE ***

The committee was made up of so called knowledgeable computer people, not real computer people, but people who think they are computer people. There were a couple of branch managers, three or four ES supervisors and a half dozen other people that were friends of the other people. The committee would meet once or twice a month or whenever they wanted to get out of their offices for a day. Usually they met at the Lansing office, as Lansing was more centrally located.

The committee would get to the meeting place in the morning about nine thirty, have to have travel time, you know, take a break about ten thirty, go to lunch a little before noon, get back about one thirty, break at three, leave for the day at four. Travel time. Why go back to the office? Closer to go home. What was accomplished? Nothing, of course. But a good time was had by all!

While the paperless committee, as it was known, was having

fun, Butch was entering applicants' information from the twenty-five elevens into the computer. Butch said to himself, "Self, why am I entering information off a hard copy when the applicant is sitting at my desk? Why can't I just enter the information directly into the computer while I'm interviewing the applicant?" Butch tried just that.

An applicant came to his desk. "Have a seat. What is your name?" As the applicant talked, Butch entered into computer, "What is your address?" Entered. "What is your education, training, experience?" And on it went until he had entered all the information during the interview. After the interview, Butch figured he saved time and saved a forest of paper.

Now Butch was not as computer literate as all the people on the paperless committee, but he found out he didn't need a twenty-five eleven to enter information into the computer. He believed, but didn't know, if the information he entered on his computer could be brought up on the computers of staff members. Butch sat down at a staff member's computer. Bingo! There it was! Any information entered on any computer in the office could be seen on all the computers in the office.

Butch wondered if he could do the same with the twenty-three sixteen. Come to find out, he could. Butch stumbled upon a way to replace both the twenty-five eleven and the twenty-three sixteen. Just happened, the paperless committee was having a meeting at the Lansing office. During one of the breaks, Butch asked Vedo, a member of the committee and former DVOW from the Lansing office, to see what he'd discovered. Vedo is, at this time, the ES supervisor at another MESC Office. After viewing and listening to Butch, Vedo's mouth fell open.

Vedo exclaimed, "I can't believe it! Do you care if I mention this to the committee?"

"No, go right ahead."

Vedo returned to the paperless committee meeting. After the meeting Butch asked Vedo, "Well, what did they think?"

Vedo, kind of dumbfounded, said, "They really didn't seem to be interested. They don't think you can number the job order forms sequentially."

"Vedo, didn't you see that it can work?"

"I guess," Vedo said. "I'll look into it more when I get back to the office." I'll look into it, is like saying the check is in the mail.

Nothing is going to happen, and with Vedo who knew less than average

about computers, Butch knew nothing was the best Vedo could do.

But Butch knew his discovery would work.

Butch showed his discovery to the other staff members, and

every one of them caught on right away. He asked the others to enter a

few twenty-five elevens directly into the system. Some were a little

nervous about their personal keyboard skills. They felt they were too

slow. Some of the interviewers had to hunt and peck. Butch

encouraged them to try anyway and they did. When the applicants were

interviewed, some of them asked why they had to fill out the twenty-

five eleven if the worker was going to type it in the computer. Good

question. Even the applicants could see the twenty-five elevens were

not needed any more. At the end of the day, they all said no matter

how slow they might be, direct entering of information was not only

faster but saved all the paper of the twenty-five eleven and twenty-three

sixteens.

One of the interviewers asked, "What's next?"

Butch said, "I need to convince Kirk," Kirk was the assistant manager at the time and really computer knowledgeable, "that we need to go paperless, to give up the twenty-five elevens and the twenty-three sixteens."

Everyone laughed. Good luck with that idea.

People, by in large, do not like change, government does not like change at all, and Kirk didn't like change most of all!

*** OUT WITH THE OLD IN WITH THE NEW ***

Butch said, "Kirk, I want to show you something." After his demonstration all Kirk could say was "Damn!"

"Well," Butch said, "what do you think? Will it work or not?"

"Sure," Kirk said.

"Good, tomorrow we can throw all the twenty-five eleven and twenty-three sixteens away." Butch started to walk away.

Kirk, all five foot three, one hundred ninety pounds of him, started running after Butch hollering, "Wait a minute, wait a minute."

Butch said, "Kirk, I thought you said it would work. Will it work or not?"

"Well, well, yes it will work, but..."

"But what?"

"You just can't throw away thousands of twenty-five elevens and hundreds of twenty-three sixteens."

"Why?"

"I don't know, you just can't. What will Melva say? Melva was the office manager."

"She'll probably kiss you for it."

"No she won't. She will probably kill me for it."

Butch said, "Let the staff enter directly for a couple of days and see how it goes."

Kirk agreed, "Okay."

A couple days later Butch told Melva, "Ask the ES interviewers what they think and if everything seems to be going okay." The answer was A-OK.

A short demonstration by Butch.

Melva was impressed, "Damn, that's great!"

"Guess we can throw those twenty-five elevens and twenty-three sixteens away."

Kirk said, "I don't know."

"We can keep the forms around for a while. We just won't use

301

them. Okay, Melva?"

Melva agreed. "Okay."

Several days went by and the paperless committee was meeting at the Lansing office again. One of the committee members, Arlene, a branch manager, approached Butch.

Arlene said, "I hear you have the answer to entering twenty-five elevens into the system?"

Butch confirmed, "Yes, twenty-three sixtteens, too."

"Will you show me?"

"Sure." Butch's demonstration only took about ten minutes or so.

"Will you come down to my office and show my ES staff how to do that?"

"Sure, but I would have to ask Melva if I could go."

Arlene assured him, "I'll ask." A few minutes later Melva and Arlene met Butch in his booth.

Melva toldhim, "Give her what she wants. How much time will you need?"

"I should make up a sheet or two as an outline," Butch said.

"The actual presentation takes about two or three hours. I'll need a day to prepare the materials."

"Could you do your presentation next week?" Arlene asked him.

"Sure."

*** OFF TO ARLENE'S OFFICE ***

Arlene asked Butch, "Are you ready?"

"As ready as I ever will be." Arlene's office was considered a small office, about five ES interviewers, no staff manager.

"I will leave you to your presentation," Arlene said. "They might be a little skeptical."

Butch looked over the staff. Not a smile. This is going to be a tough house to play to. Butch started his presentation. "I'm just like you. I am an ES interviewer out of the Lansing office. I am not a computer person at all. This is going to be a short, to the point presentation that is going to save a lot of paper, work, and time. It will make your work easier."

One of the staff members spoke up. "Getting rid of the twenty-five elevens could be a big mistake."

Butch replied, "We are not only getting rid of the twenty-five elevens but also the twenty-three sixteens."

Someone said, "Some of us are not all that computer smart. We don't type all that well either."

Butch looked around. All he could think of was Ye of little faith. "Just go along with me, humor me, ask any questions you want. If I don't know the answer, we will figure it out together." At the end of the day every one of the interviewers bought into Butch's paperless idea. One of the staff said, "It was right there all the time."

"That's right. I didn't create or invent anything. I just stumbled on the procedure and with the help of other ES interviewers in Lansing, paperless ES became a reality."

The word got back to Melva that Butch could walk on water, well maybe not on water but he was a pretty good swimmer. During the next two weeks other office managers called Melva. "Who's this guy that has the paperless program? Will you send him to our office?" The whole paperless thing with Butch put Melva in the limelight because she had *the guy* with the paperless program.

304

CHAPTER FORTY-SIX

*** NEW SHERIFF IN TOWN ***

Then came the call. The call was from the Ivory Tower, the State Office. The call was from the newly appointed Director of MESC, F. Robert Shaw, better known, not to his face, as F. Rob. F. Rob was appointed by the Governor.

The Governor and F. Rob had served in the state senate together. F. Rob, besides being a state senator, was owner of several apartments. F. Rob was, well, he was what we might call a slum lord. He had several HUD rentals. This is not to say that he did anything wrong. He just had houses that were, shall we say, built to minimum specifications and rented at the highest price HUD would pay.

It didn't hurt to be a state senator. State directors are appointees, they are not state employees. Governors have friends;

friends become directors. Most directors receive a nice salary and follow directions of a top state employee.

The top state employees are generally known as assistant directors. If the assistant director knew what he was doing, which most don't, everything would be okay. Assistant directors give the same bad information to all the appointed directors no matter if they were democrat or republican. The assistant director to F. Rob was Paul Powloski. Paul was well educated, with twenty-five years seniority with the state of Michigan.

The director before F. Rob was John Tyler. Director Tyler would go into a local office of the MESC, surrounded by his four man entourage, and would not talk to anyone but the manager, nod his head and leave. This was quite typical of directors.

F. Rob was different. He really seemed to want to know firsthand what was going on. When he was first appointed, and no one at local offices knew what he looked like, he would go to a local office, dress like a regular worker, stand in the unemployment line and talk with unemployed workers about how they were being treated at MESC and what could be done differently. MESC had some negative criticism from the general public, some warranted, most was not. People in general like to complain about government employees and government programs.

*** MR. BROWN ***

Employers would often say that the ES personnel would not respond fast enough in sending qualified applicants. Butch received a phone call from a person who said she was calling for her employer, Mr. Brown. She said he was interested in placing a job order with the MESC. Mr. Brown was not available just then but would Butch please call back about five P.M.? Butch said, "Yes." At five P.M. on the dot, Butch called Mr. Brown's office. His secretary answered the phone.

Butch asked, "Is Mr. Brown in? I am returning his call from earlier this morning."

"I'm sorry Mr. Brown just left for the day," the secretary said. "Could you call back tomorrow about eight A.M.?"

Butch told her, "Yes I will. Would you please tell Mr. Brown that I called?"

"Yes."

Next morning eight A.M. Butch called Mr. Brown. His secretary answered.

Butch said, "I am returning Mr. Brown's phone call of yesterday and the day before. Is Mr. Brown there?"

Secretary said again, "I am so sorry, he is not."

Butch was getting just a little upset. "When do you think Mr. Brown will be in?"

"I am very sure he will be in at three this afternoon."

"I will call back then."

At ten thirty Kirk, along with F. Rob, showed up at Butch's booth.

Kirk said by way of introduction, "I guess you know who this is." Butch stood to shake F. Rob's hand. As he does, Butch said, "Yes I do."

At that moment F. Rob reached for Butch's hand and said, "Hi, I'm Mr. Brown." F. Rob set Butch up. Mr. Brown's employer scheme was to see if MESC's ES staff would go the extra mile to please an employer.

Butch said, "It was one of the few tests I ever passed. What do you know, I did something right once in a row."

*** THE CALL ***

Melva answered the phone. "This is F. Rob Shaw. I hear you have an ES interviewer throwing away all the forms and entering directly into the computer. I also hear that he is going to other offices and throwing all their forms away. I wonder where he got the authority to do that? Do you know anything about this matter?"

Melva admitted that she knew what was happening and yes she gave him, Butch, the authority to do it.

F. Rob, "Great it's about time people stepped up and took the initiative to get things done. I would like to have him come to the State Office and show a few of us here what he is doing."

Melva, dumbfounded responded, "Okay. When?"

"A week from today, ten A.M."

309

Later in a staff meeting, Melva said she turned absolutely white! Everyone on the staff, including Melva, broke out in a roar. (Remember Melva was an African American.)

CHAPTER FORTY-SEVEN

*** PRESENTATION AT THE IVORY TOWER ***

Butch was escorted into a conference room and presented to F. Rob and Herman Braun, head of finance and chair of special projects for MESC. Herman was a large man, well over six feet, and over two hundred pounds, with graying, straight brown hair. He could pass for one of Hitler's generals. F. Rob introduced Braun, Paul Powloski, and four other people, who Butch didn't have the foggiest idea what they had to do with the paperless project, were also in attendance.

"This is Director Richard Davidson and Assistant Director Harlson from the Ohio Employment Office, Mr. Jack Parson, Director of the Minnesota Employment office and his assistant Paul Carson," F-Rob introduced the other four.

Butch went numb and didn't hear a word that F. Rob said for a moment or two. "Herman and I have been exchanging information with our fellow employment friends from Ohio and Minnesota. In the last couple of days we have had a few presentations on how to better administer Employment Services, make the job placement easier,

311

faster, more employer friendly. Herman and I would like you to show how you have replaced thousands of pieces of paper, not only making the job easier and faster, but also less costly."

Butch started his presentation by handing out his self-made packets with a few copies of the different computer pages. During the presentation and after a few questions were asked, Herman, the money guy asked, "How much do you think it would cost to train ES staff statewide?"

Butch thought, "How in the hell would I know?" He never gave it a thought. But he answered, "You mean every ES staff in the state?"

"Yes."

Butch said, "I haven't really thought about the cost. It wouldn't be much. If it were me setting up the training, I would use ES staff, train five or six to go to offices in their own districts. That would cut down on overnight travel and other expenses."

"How long would it take you to train the trainers?" Herman asked.

Butch answered, "One day. All on the same day."

"How long," F-Rob asked, "would it take to train the entire state after the training started?"

Butch answered, "With six trainers counting myself, we could train an office per day, the state in a month or less. I would guess the cost would be somewhere in the area of $25,000 or less, not counting the salaries of the trainers. They are on the payroll anyway."

Herman burst out laughing. "Can't be much of a program if it doesn't cost a million or so." Herman was just kidding. F. Rob was all smiles, proud of his ES interviewer from Owosso. The boys from Ohio and Minnesota were impressed.

After the presentation F. Rob met with Butch and told him to get started. Get started he did. In less than a month Butch had trained the people that would be the trainers, one from each district. In the meantime, F. Rob sent memos to all district and local office managers to cooperate one hundred percent with Butch and the paperless program.

Butch got anyone he wanted to be a trainer and any material he wanted. Butch spent a week at the Ivory Tower, State Office building in Detroit, compiling booklets for training sessions and scheduling training for local offices. The Ivory Tower was a very large building just down and across the street from, what was then General Motors World Headquarters. Butch met a lot of the big shots of MESC.

In one of the main meeting rooms, posted in a large display, were all the MESC ES state wide projects, the name of the project, the estimated cost, 2.5 million for this and 3.2 million for that, a brief description and the project leader's name. All projects headed up by the big cheeses, the big boys and big girls, director of this or director of that. The last project, Paperless Project, and there was Butch's name, cost twenty-five thousand dollars.

All the big boys and big girls would walk up and down the hallways with a scowl or frown on their faces. It seemed they were carrying a piece of paper. One day Marv, an interviewer at the Owosso office, stopped by to visit Butch in the Ivory Tower. Marv was there to be trained in testing. Butch told Marv he could walk anywhere in the building as long as he had what appeared to be a State I.D. badge and a piece of paper in his hand.

Butch was the talk of the Ivory Tower. F. Rob loved pointing to the Paperless Project every time he was in the board room.

314

*** JEALOUSY WILL GET YOU NO WHERE ***

Butch was also known in all the local offices throughout the state. Everyone in the ES world didn't care for Butch's paperless project and some didn't care that much for Butch. They might have been just a little jealous.

While Butch was presenting the paperless project at a local MESC office, the branch manager interrupted the presentation and asked Butch if he could take a break as he was wanted on the phone. The person on the phone was Debra. She was the Director of ES operations for the state of Michigan. She was one of the good ole girls. MESC was building up quite a group of good ole girls.

Butch answered the phone. "Hello, Debra, what's up?" Butch had met Debra during his travels around the state doing ES interviewer training.

She said, "You are making a lot of people look bad."

"What, how am I doing that?"

"With your paperless project. F. Rob is wondering how you came up with your project and the paperless committee didn't."

315

Actually, that was a good question. They not only looked bad, they were bad.

Not wanting to rock the boat anymore than he had, Butch asked Debra, "What do you want me to do?"

"Call your project something else would be a start."

Butch said, "Let's see, the project has already been named, it is known statewide, we have had several training sessions. Debra, I have said from the start that I have received help from several people, managers, interviewers. I will continue to give recognition to everyone."

Debra said, "Well, do what you can."

"I will do my best."

Butch now knew something else. Some time back, Butch submitted his idea of paperless to the awards committee. The State of Michigan, like private industry, had a system that allowed employees to submit suggestions that would lower costs through reduction in material and increased productivity. MESC awards could be anything from a pat on the back to five thousand dollars. At the time, Butch believed with all the paper and time his paperless project would save, he would get near the five thousand dollar mark; instead his suggestion was turned down.

Butch submitted a second suggestion addressing the issues the committee had to his first suggestion. He was turned down a second time. The committee's concerns were bogus at best. Just happens the chair of the awards committee was, you guessed it, Debra. Two other members of, gee, you guessed it again, two managers that were also on the paperless committee. Couldn't be they were afraid of how things might look? Nah, they wouldn't do that, would they?

Butch never received any award money. Debra's attempt at intimidation didn't work either. What was Debra going to do, make Butch an ES interviewer in Lansing? Remember Butch had F. Rob on his side. F. Rob was not that happy with the so called paperless committee of Debra's. He liked it when frontline personnel like Butch came up with good ideas. There were quite a few.

CHAPTER FORTY-EIGHT

*** BIG MEETING, I MEAN BIG ***

Every year MESC held a meeting where personnel from supervisor level up to F. Rob attended. Altogether there was over one hundred fifty in attendance. There would be speakers from all over the state, some from out of state, speaking on motivation and what not, all very professional with charts and videos, all very well done.

F. Rob had his assistant, Randy, call Butch and invite him to present his paperless project at the annual meeting. Butch didn't know what to think. He was flattered and scared half to death at the same time.

Butch said he would have to okay it with Kirk. Kirk was now Lansing MESC Branch Manager. Melva had recently retired. Randy asked, "Who is Kirk?"

Butch said, "He is the new Branch Manager."

"Call me back when you get the okay so we can tie up any loose ends," Randy said.

When Butch saw Kirk he said, "I just got a call from F. Rob's assistant, Randy, and he asked if I would make a presentation about paperless at the managers' meeting in Grand Rapids."

Kirk said, "Oh, I don't think you would like going to that meeting. Just a bunch of blowhards sitting around drinking and bragging."

Butch turned and walked away thinking, I guess that's a no. Butch placed a call to Randy. "I asked Kirk about me going to the managers' meeting and he seems to think I wouldn't like it or maybe it's just not a place for me."

Randy asked, "Do you want to go?"

"Sure."

Randy told him, "F. Rob wants you to be there. I'll give, what was his name, Kirk? I'll give Kirk a call. Everything will be okay."

Butch warned him, "Don't tick him off. He's my boss and I have to live with him."

"Don't worry, I'll make him think it was his idea."

Sure enough Butch and Kirk were off to the managers' meeting. The evening they arrived, a small informal dinner was served, and as Kirk said, most of the good ole boys and good ole girls sat around

319

playing cards and talking and bragging.

Butch couldn't sleep that night. He really didn't know what he was going to do. He had made up some overhead slides from the packet he used during training. There was no power point. Butch had to squeeze a two or three hour presentation into ten minutes. Talk about pulling a rabbit out of a hat.

The next morning Butch and the other presenters met in the ballroom where the banquet was going to be held. The room was large, there were round tables with white linen table clothes, eight people to a table, twenty tables, all set in a semicircle, four more tables set in the center of the room close to the stage. There was thick carpet, huge glass chandeliers from the ceiling. Nothing like this back in Byron.

The other presenters were meeting with the stage manager. They knew exactly what they wanted: "Place the spotlight over here, I will need this music played at the beginning and turn the sound down when I get to the stage." Butch thought, "Well, I can tell you what to do with the spotlight, alright, and I don't have any music! If I did, it would have to be *What a Fool Am I*."

All Butch had was an outdated overhead projector, some

homemade slides taken from his paperless project and made on a worn out copy machine. Butch was a fish out of water and he knew it.

"Sir, Sir." It was the stage manager.

Butch thought, "He must be talking to me. He's talking and looking at me.

"How do you want us to set up for your presentation?"

Butch replied, "I don't have the foggiest idea."

The stage manager just stared at Butch. Butch looked around. He actually said a prayer under his breath, "If I ever needed you, Lord, I need you now."

"Sir," it was the stage manager again.

Butch said, "Just a moment, please." Butch noticed the stage wasn't very big, twelve by fifteen feet and maybe three feet off the floor. Butch asked the stage manager, "What's that roll hanging up in back of the stage?" Stage manager said, "That is the screen we pull down if someone wants to project something."

"Good, I will need to use it. Would you put a chair beside the projector? Have the chair facing the screen." Butch continued to look around the ballroom where the white linen covered tables set in a semicircle.

Butch asked the stage manager, "Do you have a hand held mic? One that is cordless."

"Yes."

Butch all of a sudden started to relax a little. What the hell, he thought, you can only die once! Butch, talking mainly to himself, but in the direction of the stage manager, "What I will do is stand in the middle of this semi-circle and make my presentation somewhat like a standup comedian, while my assistant will run the overhead. How much time did you say I have?"

"You will be the fifth presenter. You will have ten minutes. I will be off stage over there." he pointed. "I will give you the one minute signal, the thirty second signal, the last ten seconds, and music will start low and get louder to let you know you're done."

Butch said, "Now all I have to do is find an assistant."

At dinner Butch asked Kirk if he would help him run the projector and change the slides. Kirk said yes. Kirk was an alright guy, just a little jealous of Butch's new-found fame.

Butch told him, "I have the slides in order and lettered. When I say Slide B shows such and such, just make the exchange."

About that time F. Rob came over to Butch and Kirk's table and shook Butch's hand and says, "Ready for your presentation?"

Butch lied, "Oh sure, no problem." No problem? Butch didn't eat three bites of food. He could hardly breathe. His fingers were going numb. No problem.

F. Rob said, "I think I might be a little nervous if it were me. I know you will do just fine."

Butch thought, "Oh great, that's a relief. I think I will just take one of these chicken bones and swallow it and choke to death. That would be easier."

The lights in the ballroom started to dim. That was Butch's signal to get ready for his presentation. Off to one side in the dark with just a small flashlight stood those mighty six hundred, well, maybe not the mighty six hundred but the seven or eight presenters for the night. Butch noticed something, they all seemed to be just as nervous as he was, maybe not quite that nervous. Butch couldn't remember a thing, hands sweaty, heart pumping, this was a big deal to Butch. All those bigshots. Prayer, "Lord don't let me make a fool of myself."

You're next, someone pulled at Butch's arm. His legs felt like lead. "Our next presenter is..." Butch really didn't hear his name.

Butch stepped out of the darkness with the mic in his right hand, he heard a nice applause. Butch nodded and waved politely to the room full of people. Quick prayer, "Lord, I see only one set of footprints in the sand. Is that you carrying me? If it is, for crying out loud, don't drop me."

When Butch got to his mark, he stopped. Butch could not make out a soul with the spotlight shining, it sort of blurred everyone out. Butch thought, just like at a basketball game you can hear the sound of people, here you can't see the people. Butch said he felt like a Las Vegas performer about to perform. He was starting to relax a little, pushing some hair off his forehead and thinking, Frank Sinatra eat your heart out! He nodded once more and turned toward the stage, and there sitting at the projector, all five feet whatever, all one hundred ninety pounds, slightly slumped forward with his back to the audience facing the screen, was Kirk.

Butch said, "Kirk, you put up the wrong screen!" Kirk quickly made the correction. Butch looked at the audience. "Well, you can take the boy from the farm, but you just can't take the farm from the boy." The place broke up laughing, even Kirk. At the conclusion of his presentation the music started very softly, perfect timing. The lights came on, and the applause was very loud.

As Butch started to walk off, Manny from Arizona, a newly hired right hand man to F. Rob, stood up and motioned for Butch to come to his table.

Manny told him, "Great job, great job."

Butch thanked him and started to leave when F. Rob stood up and motioned for Butch to join him. Shaking Butch's hand he said, "Sit here," pointing to a chair beside him. "Sit here for the remainder of the presentations. "You were great, the best! You should go on stage." Butch thought to himself, everybody has their fifteen minutes of fame and I just had mine. Butch never made it to the stage, but he did make a few ES training videos.

Butch was now really becoming the *go to guy*. He was already on different committees. The computer system ES used was called Magic and was going to be updated. One of the committees was the Magic 2000. The Magic 2000 started late, quit early, and took long lunch hours. Sounds a little like another committee we talked about. Butch would look in the mirror once in a while and ask, "Have I become one of them?" Nah! They acted stupid and didn't know it. If Butch acted stupid, at least he knew it.

The hospitality committee was one of the best. A state senator from the Upper Peninsula of Michigan got his shirt in a knot because the resorts in upper Michigan were hiring Jamaicans to work in the resorts instead of locals. He felt that locals could do as good a job. The owners of the resorts, being more intelligent than the state senator, didn't fight the accusation at all. They welcomed the state or anyone else to find anyone to fulfill their needs.

The government did what government does best. They throw money at the problem and formed a committee. How nice. The MESC was selected to conduct the investigation and report back. Guess who was one of the committee members? You got it, good old Butch and the girls. Remember the good ole girls from the paperless committee? It just never ends.

The resort owners being ten times smarter than the state legislature, suggested that the committee members go to the different resorts, stay a day or two at the three to five hundred dollar a night hotels, and eat at their five star restaurants. I mean you have to know what kind of atmosphere the worker will be working in, don't you? This was done at the expense of the resort owners, it did not cost the state one penny, except transportation and salary. What the heck, the committees' salary had to be paid anyway, right? All other expenses, room, food, taxi service was paid by the resort owners, who probably took it as a tax deduction. The mission was to see why Michigan born and bred workers couldn't replace the imported Jamaican workers. Let's see, the Jamaican workers worked in the ski lodges and aboard cruise ships in the winter and came to Michigan and other northern states in the summers. The Jamaicans were pros at spoiling people.

One evening after being spoiled all day, Butch and the girls went to a bar in the hotel. Hotel rules state that a man must wear a tie in order to be served. Butch had taken his tie off and left it in his room. Butch ordered a drink. The Jamaican waiter, with a gasp, said, "Yes sir, I will bring you your drink." A minute later the waiter returned with the drink and a tie and simply said, "Here you are sir, your drink and tie, you forgot."

At dinner one of the girls complained in a low voice that she wished she had ordered creme brulee instead of the strawberry shortcake she ordered. In a flash the Jamaican waiter appeared from nowhere and said, "I'm sorry for the error, and gave her creme brulee. Could you see a laid off factory worker, construction worker, farmer, or a person that never really held a regular job doing this kind of work for the pay the Jamaicans were getting? Not in your life! By the way it never did happen. Many were sent, few served.

CHAPTER FORTY-NINE

*** LIFE IS GOOD--NOT SO FAST ***

Butch has two children, a daughter, Sherri, and a son, Cary. Sherri was nearly a perfect child to raise. She always did what she was asked. She received excellent grades in school, played in the school band and was first chair, number one flutist. Sherri received a challenge from the number two flutist. Anyone could challenge the person ahead of them to move up in the pecking order. This was done once a month. Sherri lost her number one seat. Butch said to her, "That's okay. You can challenge her next month."

Sherri, "No, I don't think so. "

"Why?"

"That's all she has."

"What do you mean, that's all she has?"

"She lives way out in the country. She doesn't come into town much, doesn't take part in anything. Being in the band is all she really has." Sherri never challenged for number one again, but Sherri never lost second seat. She was in the flag corp, a cheerleader, and very popular and active in school as well as church. Sherri went on to graduate from Michigan State University and became a teacher for children with special needs. Only a special person can do that.

CHAPTER FIFTY

*** IN GOD'S HANDS ***

Cary was a small to average size kid, about five feet five and weighed one hundred twenty-five pounds. He was a very good athlete, with a lot of athleticism. He played two years junior varsity football at one hundred ten pounds. and varsity baseball. He was a four-year varsity wrestler. As a wrestler Cary qualified for the state tournament twice, won a district championship and was the first wrestler to win one hundred or more matches in a career at Byron High School. He was small, but definitely not a wimp.

Cary, like his sister, was a very good student. After high school graduation, he was off to THE UNIVERSITY OF MICHIGAN. Like most college kids Cary would come home to get clothes washed, get more spending money and check in. On one occasion he approached Butch and said, "There is something wrong with me."

Butch with his normal weird wit said, "Well, I've known that for some time."

"No, I mean here in this area." Cary pointed to his private area.

"We all have problems in that area, Cary."

"No, I have a lump, a bump, a growth on my right testicle." All of a sudden humor is gone and seriousness sets in.

Butch asked, "Are you sure, does it hurt?"

"Yes, I am sure. No, it doesn't hurt."

"We need to get you to a doctor." Butch never wanting to avoid a problem led Cary into the house and explained the situation to Diana. Diana made a call to the doctor's office. After she explained the condition, an appointment was made for the following day. The family doctor made his examination, he called in the general surgeon that does the surgery for the clinic that Butch's family went to. Both concur, Cary needed surgery and the sooner the better. The doctors said it could be testicular cancer. Only a lab report would determine for sure.

332

Butch asked the doctor, "When can you schedule the surgery?"

The family doctor, "The middle of next week." This was less than a week after Cary told Butch about his problem. Time is of the essence. Both the family doctor and surgeon said this type of cancer was very curable if caught in time and you move fast.

Butch turned to Cary, "Okay?"

Cary said, "What choice do I have?"

"None really," the family doctor stated.

Cary asked, "What's going to happen?"

The two doctors looked at each other, then at Butch, then to Cary. "We are going to have to remove your testicle."

Oh that sounds just great! Cary has just turned twenty, his whole life in front of him, and you want to cut off his right testicle.

"We will be able to put in a prosthesis, the surgery should have no effect on your ability to produce children."

Well, that's much better. That's like telling someone that you are going to cut off their nose, but it won't interfere with their breathing.

333

After the surgery, the surgeon entered the waiting area where Butch and Diana were. He didn't look happy.

Butch asked, "What did you find?"

Surgeon said, "I removed the testicle and prepared it for the lab. I would say Cary has testicular cancer."

If you have never had a doctor say "You have cancer" you don't know the feeling that comes over you.

"We won't know for sure until we get the lab report."

Butch asked, "When will that be and what's next?"

"As soon as we get the lab report Dr. Manne the family doctor, will call you in for consultation on what you might want to do next."

"And what might that be?" Butch wanted to know.

Surgeon said, "Let's take it one step at a time."

Days passed. Finally it was time to meet with Dr. Manne.

Dr. Manne announced, "Cary has testicular cancer."

"What's next?" Again, Butch wanted to know.

Dr. Manne told him, "I'll get an appointment with an oncologist, a cancer doctor."

Butch ordered, "Make it with one that you would send your son to."

Dr. Manne said, "That would be Dr. Sanborn. His main office is in Lansing, which would be convenient for you. We will try to make the appointment right now if you can wait."

"We will wait." Butch said. Dr. Manne's office made the appointment with Dr. Sanborn for three days hence.

Dr. Sanborn, after all the hellos, and shaking hands, "Well, Cary, you do have testicular cancer. Now what are we going to do about it? One, you can start chemo and radiation, along with blood work ups and after a few months we can hope all is well, or you can have exploratory surgery. They will go in and remove some of your lymph nodes, look around, send samples to the lab to see if there is any cancer there, along with sending in blood work to see if there is any cancer there. By the way, your last blood work ups look great." Finally a little good news. "That doesn't mean you're cancer free, it just means right now everything looks good in your blood. There still could be cancer cells floating around."

Well the little good news didn't last too long.

"Which would you recommend?" Butch asked.

"That's not for me to say. Cary is young, in very good heath, other than this cancer thing. Good shape."

Butch turned his son, "Cary, what do you want to do? Think it over a little first."

Dr. Sanborn reminded them, "You can think it over, but not too long."

Cary said, "Let's decide now. Let's go with the surgery."

Dr. Sanborn then said, "Next, let's select a surgeon. We have a half dozen or so that are quite capable of doing this kind of surgery and doing it well."

Cary decided on Dr. Shore, the fastest knife in town, gets in, gets out, and is top notch.

Butch and Cary met with Dr. Shore in four days. Things were moving fast and that was good. Dr. Shore wasn't long with formalities. Dr. Shore was a no nonsense guy, straight to the point, bar nothing, just the way both Butch and Cary liked it. "Cary you got cancer, we need to operate remove your lymph nodes, send them to the lab so we can find out where we stand. This is how the operation will go. I will cut you from here to here." He put his index finger on Cary's sternum and ran it down as far as he could go. "I'll open you up, look around at all you got, remove your lymph nodes and anything else that looks suspicious, close you up and wait for the lab reports. Oh, yes, there is one more thing, I need to mention, it rarely happens, it never has happened with me. When I make the incision at the bottom, I could cut some of the nerve ends that affect you getting an erection. Like I say, I have never had that problem, but I need to let you know."

Now let's review. What we have here is a young man twenty years old, a Christian young man, going to college, working summers to help pay his way. In the last three weeks you tell him he has testicular cancer, remove his right testicle, tell him he has to be cut from stem to stern, have his lymph nodes removed, look around to see if there isn't something else you might remove and, by the way, as an afterthought, you might not be able to have an erection. Can't see any problems here?

The night before the operation Cary had a lifelong friend, Jeff, over for company. Butch could see that pending surgery was weighing heavily on Cary, although Cary was covering it up pretty well.

Butch said, "Cary, why don't you and I go for a little drive.

You don't mind do you, Jeff?"

Jeff said, "Oh no, go ahead."

Butch felt he should talk with Cary to try to make him feel better. This was something Butch had been good at most of his life. Talking, counseling, even when he was a teenager. It was getting late, around ten at nnight, not much traffic. Butch saw a little park that was near the house and pulled over, stopped the car, put the car in park, and looked at Cary, and lost it. He broke down sobbing, not crying, sobbing, tears rolling down his cheeks, couldn't catch his breath, couldn't speak a recognizable word, type crying. Butch put his arms across the steering wheel and flopped his head on his arms. A few seconds passed and Cary put his left hand very gently on Butch's right shoulder. Butch looked up into Cary's eyes.

Cary said with a very soft but firm voice, "It's going to be alright, Dad, really it's going to be alright." Not a quiver in his voice, not a tear in his eyes, just a look of comfort for his father. "It's all in God's hands and he's going to take care of me." What faith! What belief Cary has! Not in his father, not the doctors, God would see him through and see him through HE did!

Next morning, after the operation was complete, Dr. Shore walked into the waiting area and announced, "He is doing great. You will be able to see him in his room in a couple of hours. They will let you know when and what room. I took out the lymph nodes. And had a good look at the other organs. From strictly a visual look, everything looks good. Of course..."

Butch said, "Yes we know, you won't know anything until the lab reports come in on the lymph nodes and blood."

Dr. Shore added, "Cary should be able to go home in three, four days. I'll see him in two weeks to have the stitches out and go over the lab reports. My secretary will set up the appointment."

Two weeks later at Dr. Sanborn the oncologist's office he said, "Well Cary, some very good news. Your lab report came back clean, no cancer reported in your blood. Your general health is very good."

Butch asked, "No chemo, no radiation?"

Dr. Sanborn, "Not for now."

"What's next?" Cary asked.

Dr. Sanborn said, "Cary, you are still going to have to have blood work ups over a period of time. If at any time any cancer cells show up you will have to go to chemo and radiation."

Cary wanted to know, "For how long, when do we start?"

"Over a period of about five years," Dr. Sanborn explained, "We start in a week. You can go to a lab that is just a few blocks from where you live. I'll give you a schedule before you leave. I'll also call you in for a visit during the next year. The schedule will look like this. A blood draw once a week for four weeks, then every two weeks for three months, once a month for six months, once every three months for a year. Then twice a year for two years, I recommend once a year for at least three years. If nothing shows up, and I mean nothing, we say you're cancer free."

Cary said, "That's a long time to wait."

Dr. Sanborn admitted, "Yes it is, however the longer you go, the better it will be."

CHAPTER FIFTY-ONE

*** GRADUATION DAY ***

Cary graduated from the University of Michigan with a degree in accounting. After graduating jobs were not easy to find, so Cary took a job in an optometrist's office getting only slightly over minimum wage. He lived with Butch and Diana for a while, bought a small economy car, and later moved into a cheap apartment. After a few months Cary was hired into the state of Michigan Treasury Department, governmental audit division.

After fourteen months, Cary came to Butch and said he would like to buy a house. Cary was not married at this time. Butch asked him how much did he think he would have to pay for a house. Cary thought about seventy-five thousand dollars, give or take a little.

Butch said, "Well Cary, you will need at least ten percent down.

How much money do you have?"

He said, "Fifteen thousand dollars." Cary had saved fifteen thousand dollars in fourteen months.

Cary lived the same life style that he lived before working at Treasury and he banked the rest. He had to travel all over Michigan doing audits and was paid for mileage, which he saved. He was paid expense money for breakfast, lunch and dinner, way more than needed, as he didn't eat breakfast, and ate fast food for lunch, and ate a light dinner. Cary bought his first house for sixty-five thousand dollars and sold it a few years later for seventy-five thousand. Cary is now forty-seven years old, married to a women with three sons which Cary adopted. He is a CPA and a supervisor of governmental auditing with the state of Michigan.

When Cary first started working with the state, Butch suggested he take a special class to prepare to be a CPA. To be a CPA in Michigan the requirements are two years apprenticeship in an approved accounting program and pass a very difficult written test. Cary complained hard and long that he didn't want any more schooling. Butch mentioned this several times with the same response from Cary.

342

Why would you listen to your father whose occupation is helping people obtain employment and training?

A few weeks after Butch's last attempt, Cary called him. "I was talking with my supervisor the other day and he said it might be a good idea if I were to pursue classes to become a CPA."

Butch paused, "Sounds like a great idea!" Cary laughed.

CHAPTER FIFTY-TWO

*** RETIREMENT? ***

Now is life good? After all the rough years anything has to be an improvement. Like a lot of life lessons, they're worth a million dollars to have experience, but you wouldn't take a dime to do them over.

There were big changes in government programs. Something had to give. Too much tax, too much give away. Most government programs took some kind of hit. MESC was no exception.

Early retirements at most government agencies in Michigan were offering very nice retirement packages. Of course, years later the government who made all sorts of promises wanted to take back their promise, saying they just didn't have the money. Governments had mismanaged the budget and wanted retired government employees to pay for it. Nevertheless, retirement sounded nice. Cary, now a CPA, crunched the numbers and said, "Well dad, if you want to work for five dollars and seventy cents an hour, continue to work, if not retire."

With Diana, the choice was simple. Diana's job was horrible at best. More and more people on welfare, caseloads that were top heavy with one hundred fifty clients per load were now more than two hundred and getting worse.

Both Butch and Diana retired. Butch says it took Diana one day to adjust to retirement, not so for Butch. He really liked his job at MESC. Oh, there were days he wanted to stomp on the ground and say damn. Butch really believed he and the others at MESC were providing a service to the general public and especially to employers.

Retirement parties were held by the dozens. All the people with experience were leaving like rats from a sinking ship. A few years earlier, an early retirement was offered and over twenty-five branch managers, dozens of supervisors and even more experienced employees retired. This offer was going to claim more!

Butch was invited to a retirement party the girls were having. But the big question was what was going to happen to MESC?

Today was the day the answer was coming down. A big, big meeting was being held in Lansing. Jan, who was the recently appointed District Manager, was at the meeting where the news was being released and was going to be a little late

345

The party started at noon and at twelve twenty in popped Jan. She was a little spitfire of a person. She held nothing back. "They're going to eliminate ES altogether except for service to veterans. Service to vets is a federal law. They're only going to have three UI offices in the state, one in Detroit, one in Saginaw, one in Grand Rapids. Everything will be done by phone and computer."

Talk about a formula for a screw up, that was it and sadly it still is. With no accountability on the part of the applicant, who's watching the chicken coop? No one. You can register your resume online and an employer can go online and see it. Unfortunately few applicants do. You could go to a so called employment center and they will help you. Employers can list their jobs online and applicants can view them. Butch has news for you, it doesn't work! Butch knows this because he and a MESC coworker worked at a hiring center for over five years.

Butch said to Jan, "I am glad I am retiring." Just a few weeks before Jan tried to talk Butch into staying. Life has to be good now. Retirement! A new retiree asked an older retiree about retirement, and the advice was, "You need to find something to do." You could repeat that a million times. It is a true statement. Don't take it lightly.

How are you going to fill in forty hours a week that you once filled working? You may not have liked your job, but it did take up some time. Most men have a difficult time the first year or two. Women somehow seem to fill in the time easier.

*** MOVE TO THE COUNTRY ***

Butch and Diana retired. They wanted to move from Lansing back to Shiawassee County, more their old stomping ground. They started to look for a place in Owosso. Owosso was close to the hospital, doctors, dentists, and other necessities. This becomes more important the older you get. Owosso is the hub of Shiawassee County with fifteen thousand residents. There are restaurants, supermarkets, and shopping. Good old Walmart! Will he get a bonus for mentioning Walmart? There, he did it again.

Butch says he got pretty tired watching the grass grow, hoping the grass got long enough to mow. Maybe if he mowed real slow he could take two days instead of one. Bored beyond the beyond!

CHAPTER FIFTY-THREE

*** OUT OF RETIREMENT ***

Just about the time Butch was ready to throw himself in front of a fast moving train, he got a phone call from Debra. You remember Debra. She was the one who called Butch during one of his paperless presentations, and said he was making some people look bad. Remember she was on the paperless committee and sat on the MESC rewards program?

A phone call came out of the blue a month or so after the retirements. A new program was started. Throw a lot of money at the problem and create a new bureaucracy, called Michigan Workers.

The idea was great. The implementation stunk as it usually does. The governor wanted to have a one stop shop where citizens with needs could go to one building for referrals to employment, for unemployment benefits, welfare, veterans services and many other services. One place to fill out one application and be referred directly to the people you need for each application. Sounds good. Most of the personnel staffing at Michigan Workers were not really employment people. Honest, hardworking, well intended, maybe.

What Michigan Workers needed was a statewide computer program

to store their applicants' applications and employer information. I wonder

where they could get something like that? Oh, the old MESC ES Magic

computer programs. They really did work quite well. And the people

at Michigan Workers realized that and wanted to obtain Magic. Good

idea.

What was needed now was someone to train the new statewide

staff on how to put the Magic system to use. Enter Debra. Debra was a

very intelligent person, former MESC large office branch manager,

head of employment service, and very computer literate, especially

knowledgeable about the Magic system.

Michigan Workers Program very wisely contacted Debra and

asked if she could put together a training program to train personnel in

the twenty-five or twenty-six Michigan Workers Program locations

throughout the state. They also wanted Debra to do the training.

Michigan Workers needed the training complete as soon as possible.

Debra said okay, she would need to hire a few people to help her.
She had two weeks to put the training together and approximately eight
weeks to complete the training and one week to clean up any loose
ends. The deal was made. Hence, the phone call from Debra.

"Hi, Debra, what's up?"

Debra explained the Michigan Workers proposal and asked
Butch if he would like to do the training. Butch is not a computer geek
at all. He reminded Debra of that fact.

Debra said, "You may not be a true computer person but no one
knows Magic any better than you do and you are a good trainer."

Butch said, "Okay, where and when?"

Debra added, "By the way, the other trainer will be Dave
Wheelmen." Dave was a former branch manager and a computer
person. "We will meet at the MESC office in Lansing or what's left of
it at nine next Monday."

Butch said, "I'll be there."

"Don't you want to know how much money you're going to
make?"

"Debra, I am so bored, I'll pay you to work."

"The pay is sixty dollars an hour."

Butch had to reach down his throat to get the phone he just swallowed. "How much did you say?"

Debra laughed out loud. "I said sixty dollars an hour, plus mileage, plus motels, plus meals." Butch thought he died and had gone to heaven.

After two weeks of prep time, everything was going just fine. Seven weeks in and a phone call came from Debra. Michigan Workers Program has decided they do not want to use the Magic system, they are going with America's Job Bank.

Butch asked, "America's Job Bank? That's almost as good as Magic. Magic is a better system and is already set up to go."

Debra agreed, "I know, but that's what they want and that's what they're going to get. They do want us to complete the last week of training along with the wrap up. That's not all. They want us to do the America's Job Bank training, too. That will be one week prep time, six weeks of training, one week wrap up. Not as much money either, just forty dollars an hour. Same expenses." Debra laughed.

351

"I can't believe it!" Butch said. "Finish Magic, startup America's Job bank, how stupid! What a waste of money!"

Debra said, "I just do what I'm told, mission complete."

Michigan Workers Program employees were trained in a program they would never use and cost thousands of dollars.

CHAPTER FIFTY-FOUR

*** YET ANOTHER JOB ***

Life is good. Three weeks passed since the last training and wrap up session for Michigan Workers.

A phone call from Shiawassee Health Department.

Butch said, "This is who? The Shiawassee Health Department? Am I going to die?"

"No, Mr. Stinsen would like to talk to you about employment."

"Okay"

"Hi, I'm George Stinsen. I've been talking with a couple of people at the Chamber of Commerce meetings. Your name keeps coming up as a person that knows quite a bit about employment. The Health Department received a two year contract to administer the Work Now program for Shiawassee County. We have been providing service to people on welfare for about two months. I feel we have taken on more than we can chew. I would like to talk with you about helping us with the employer contact part of our program. This seems to be the area that we lack experience the most. Would you be interested in a part time job in this area?"

"Sounds like something I could be interested in."

George asked, "Could you come to the Health Department say tomorrow morning at ten?"

Butch said, "'I'll be there."

At the meeting at the Health Department with George the next day, he said, "I'll get right to the point. We are health service people, not employment people. We bid on the contract to provide employment service to the people on welfare. We did this to keep three or four of our people from being laid off. We really didn't know the ins and outs of employment. Sounded easy enough, get jobs, send people to them. The part that seems to be the most difficult is getting employers to list jobs. We've been told this is an area that you are good at."

"I have had a lot of experience in that area and enjoy meeting with employers."

"I'm not sure if it would be a forty hour a week job or not."

"Good, I would rather work two or three days a week anyway."

"What kind of a salary would you need?"

Butch laughed. "That's funny. I always tell applicants when

354

they go on a job interview to either know what the job pays or have a figure in mind ahead of time. I haven't given it a thought."

"How would fifteen dollars an hour to start and work three days a week?"

"Sounds great if those three days were Tuesday, Wednesday, Thursday."

"Deal."

Life is good again. Work three days, off four. Not for long, however, three days turned into five. Butch took on a job-seeking skills workshop, teaching applicants how to write resumes, cover letters, interview, as well as did some job referrals.

At the end of the first year, George called a meeting of the Worker First staff. George said, "I am sorry to say the Health Department did not bid for a second year on the Worker First program. There will be a new provider at the end of the month." George went on, "The new provider is Invest in People Inc., out of Flint. They have been providing Worker First and other employment service programs for some time. Mr. Michael Hernadez, owner and president, along with Mr. Mott Dezegler, also of Invest in People Inc., would like to meet with all of you to make a short transition. I said I thought that would be okay. Mr. Hernadez and Mr. Dezegler would like to meet tomorrow, if that is okay with all of you." Everyone nodded okay.

Next day Mr. Michael Hernadez, Mott Dezegler, and a Worker First employee from Invest in People Inc. spent the first couple of hours going over the procedures the Health Department used for Worker First.

Butch just sort of sat around thinking he might as well go home. Then Michael asked Butch if he would step outside where he could have a smoke. Outside Michael and Mott asked Butch if he wouldn't mind managing the Worker First program for them. Michael said all the clerical would be handled by a Worker First staff person from Invest in People main office. Butch would handle employer contacts, job seeking skills work shop, referrals, and the like. It would definitely be a forty hour a week job. After a little more smoothing by Michael and Mott, Butch said yes.

Butch would be responsible for the job placements of four hundred welfare participants. The number changed very little over a period of time. Some left the program, others entered. Four hundred is a very small number when compared to large cities. Small or large, all

356

are governed by the same rules and same mission, put people on welfare to work. Sounds like a good idea.

There were a large number of welfare recipients, and I mean large. There were second and even third generations on welfare who were completely healthy, capable people and not working.

There were about fifteen participants in each of Butch's job seeking skill classes. Butch would ask, "How many here smoke one pack of cigarettes a day or more?" Typically seventy-five per cent would answer yes. "How many will drink one six pack or more in a week?" One third answered they did. "How many will rent two or more videos a week?" Ninety percent said they did. Again the percentages will vary, but not much. Butch's reply, "Don't. We're talking well over two thousand dollars out of pocket money. You would have to earn more than that before taxes. Two thousand dollars can go a long way toward rent, heat, electricity and food. Let's not get into drugs."

The participants would complain. They would say, "You don't want us to have any fun." Butch's response was "You're right. When you are on welfare, receiving tax payers' money, you need only the bare necessities. When you are off welfare, smoke as much as you want,

357

drink what you want, and watch as many videos as you want."

Then the big decision again. Butch decided to retire. There was a big party which Michael Hernadez did not attend. He sent a fruit basket with Motty. Never a phone call, not even a card, nothing. Butch ran Invest in People First five years for Michael, meeting or exceeding every goal, hiring, firing. Butch did it all. When he left People First he left a staff of very experienced people. Michael hired a person to replace him who had next to no experience and he paid her seven dollar an hour more. She left People First in two years. Michael always told Butch he was "falling on hard times" and couldn't increase Butch's or anyone else's salary.

CHAPTER FIFTY-FIVE

*** REAL RETIREMENT ***

Finally life is good! Butch and Diana spend four and a half months a year in south Florida in a mobile home park right on the Atlantic Ocean. It's nice, boring, but nice. If you are around any of the shuffleboard courts from Hollywood, Florida to Palm Beach, you might see Butch. His new thing is playing shuffleboard tournaments. He tours with a friend and pro shuffler from Ohio. Butch likes Tom, anyway, Buckeye or not. Butch still meets and talks with everyone. He just can't stop being the interviewer, always talking with the residents in the park. They're from everywhere, New York, California, Pennsylvania, Maryland, Kentucky, Ohio, Illinois, Minnesota, from all walks of life. Let us not forget our friends from Canada. Some of the best outdoor shuffleboard players are the French Canadians. They have a different view on life. Interesting!